Real Food
from your
Wok

Carol Palmer

foulsham
LONDON • NEW YORK • TORONTO • SYDNEY

foulsham

The Publishing House, Bennetts Close,
Cippenham, Berkshire, SL1 5AP, England

*To my dear husband Phil and
my children Emma and Joe*

ISBN 0-572-02511-4

Copyright © 2001 W. Foulsham & Co. Ltd.

Originally published as *Quick and Easy Stir-fry Cookbook*

Printed in Great Britain by The Bath Press, Bath

CONTENTS

INTRODUCTION

My experience of stir-frying dates back to my years as a home economics student living away from home for the first time with a fellow student in very basic digs. She bought me a wok for my twenty-first birthday and this became one of our few pieces of cooking equipment. Grants being small, we would scour the supermarkets and markets of East Croydon for bargains to feed our healthy appetites. As a consequence, practically all our meals were stir-fried. We didn't just survive, we thrived! Both cooking and eating were enjoyable; we never tired of our experiments but were spurred on to develop further ideas, which we practised on each other, friends and family. Many years on, we still visit each others' homes and don't feel inhibited by producing our woks from the cupboard to stir-fry the evening meal. Perhaps it was this early experience in my cooking life that showed me the versatility of stir-frying as a method of cooking. Yet to most people 'stir-frying' still conjures up a picture of the cook vigorously tossing an array of Chinese vegetables in a wok – an image that doesn't do it justice. It is simply a method of cooking that involves the frequent, not constant, stirring of ingredients in a small amount of very hot oil in either a wok or a large heavy-based frying pan (skillet).

Stir-frying may have originated in China as a means of cooking quickly and efficiently when fuel was scarce, but stir-fry dishes do not have to be Chinese in their origin or make-up. This book aims to show the enthusiastic and adventurous cook how to stir-fry a vast range of savoury and sweet dishes with a worldwide theme that may not necessarily be associated with stir-frying. The ingredients used are readily available and generally modestly priced. Like all stir-fry recipes, these are simple to follow and quick to prepare. However, you will find that they lend themselves equally well to both the family dinner table and the supper party menu.

YOUR STIR-FRY STORECUPBOARD

If you keep a storecupboard of basic items to hand, it is easy to put together something more interesting than beans on toast when you are in a hurry or when you have forgotten to dash out to the shops in your lunch hour!

It is always more efficient to shop with a list, rather than hoping you'll remember everything; and you tend to spend less too. Keep a shopping list handy in the kitchen so that you can jot down any items you have used or jars and packets that are running low. It saves checking through the cupboards before you go shopping.

CANS, BOTTLES AND PACKETS

◇ Borlotti beans
◇ Red kidney beans
◇ Mushrooms
◇ Sweetcorn (corn)
◇ Tomatoes
◇ Anchovies
◇ Honey
◇ Groundnut (peanut) oil
◇ Oyster sauce
◇ Red (bell) peppers or pimientos
◇ Dry sherry
◇ Cornflour (cornstarch)
◇ Long-grain rice
◇ Brown sugar

HERBS, SPICES AND SEASONINGS

◇ Dried herbs, including oregano and thyme
◇ Spices, including cayenne pepper, chilli powder, ground cinnamon, ground cumin, Chinese five-spice powder and paprika
◇ Salt and black peppercorns
◇ Garlic purée (paste) or lazy garlic
◇ Lemon juice
◇ Soy sauce
◇ Stock (bouillon) cubes
◇ Thai fish sauce
◇ Tomato purée (paste)
◇ Balsamic vinegar
◇ Wine vinegar
◇ Worcestershire sauce

FREEZER STANDBYS

◇ Chicken breasts or portions
◇ Minced (ground) beef or lamb
◇ White fish fillets such as cod or whiting
◇ Prawns (shrimp)
◇ Baby sweetcorn (corn)
◇ Pitta bread
◇ Chopped herbs, including parsley and basil

VEGETABLES

◇ Carrots
◇ Celery
◇ Garlic
◇ Green or red (bell) peppers
◇ Onions
◇ Shallots
◇ Spring onions (scallions)

STIR-FRY TECHNIQUES

There are few rules for stir-frying, but to get the best results from these recipes you should take note of the following guidelines.

THE UTENSILS

A wok or large heavy-based frying pan (skillet) can be used and in some cases a large heavy-based saucepan. Woks are ideal as their depth means more food can be accommodated than in a frying pan and there is less risk of it being spilled when tossed in the oil. Also, their shape means less oil is required and the heat is rapidly distributed over the surface which aids the cooking process. Woks are traditionally round-based although flat-based ones suitable for use on electric cookers are now available. The round-based woks are really safe to use only on a gas hob. If you have decided to buy a wok, choose a deep-sided one as large as you can accommodate and as heavy as possible, preferably made from carbon steel.

For stirring, metal stir-fry spatulas are available. However, there is no need to go out and buy one of these; a long-handled metal fish slice or spatula or even a metal spoon will do the job just as well.

THE METHOD

The key to effective stir-frying is to have all the ingredients prepared first so that you can concentrate on the cooking process and have no need to leave the pan. The second important step is to ensure that the wok or pan is heated until very hot before adding the oil. Next, add the oil and gently swirl it around the pan to ensure that all areas are coated, thus preventing sticking and making sure all pieces of food are subjected to the same temperature. The pan should be nearly smoking before you add the food; test the temperature with one piece of food first before adding the full quantity. If cooking garlic, ginger or chillies first, it is best if the oil is not quite this hot or they will burn and turn bitter. When you are confident that the oil is the correct temperature, proceed with the recipe, adding the ingredients to the pan as directed and gently tossing them in the hot oil. Remember, it is not essential to stir constantly; in fact for some ingredients such as meat it is important to allow it to spend time in contact with the pan surface so that it browns and cooks before stirring further. Move the food from the centre of the pan to the sides to ensure even cooking. Stir-fried food should not be greasy if it has been cooked correctly in the right amount of oil and it should have slightly more bite than food cooked by conventional methods.

THE FOOD

Generally, most foods can be stir-fried, but the amount of time required will vary with the texture and density of the individual food. It is essential that ingredients are cut into fine small pieces or strips of about the same size so that the hot oil penetrates and quickly cooks the food. Large pieces would take too long to cook and could end up greasy and unappetising. It is best to use the leaner, more tender cuts of meat as stir-frying is too rapid a method of cooking to tenderise tougher meat adequately. Always ensure that meat is cut across the grain to prevent toughness. Each recipe describes how the ingredients should be cut but generally where it says the meat should be cut into fine strips, these should be no thicker than 5 mm/¼ in and 5–7.5 cm/2–3 in long. If using meat from your freezer, it is very easy to slice thinly before it defrosts completely. Fish pieces should be slightly thicker as, like some fruits and cake, it has a delicate texture and requires a certain degree of care in stir-frying. Gentle stirring and a short cooking time should prevent the food from disintegrating. In some cases it may be necessary to blanch or parboil ingredients before stir-frying to soften them slightly, but details for this or other specific preparation techniques are given in the individual recipes.

THE OIL

It is important to use oil that does not break down at high temperatures. Groundnut (peanut) oil is ideal as it has a mild, pleasant flavour; however, this can prove rather expensive if you are planning to do a lot of stir-frying and is rather high in saturated fats. Corn oil, sunflower oil and most blended vegetable oils are cheaper and suitable for stir-frying and a healthier option as their saturated fat content is much lower.

Once the basic preparations for stir-frying have been carried out, you can proceed to conjure up untold delights from your wok or frying pan (skillet). The recipes in this book illustrate just how easy it is to stir-fry the most impressive dishes and will leave you wanting to experiment further with this quick and easy method of cooking.

NOTES ON THE RECIPES

◇ All cooking times given in this book are approximate and depend upon the heat source, size of pieces of food, and the cooking utensil used. Adjust the cooking time accordingly to ensure the food is adequately cooked but remember the vegetables should retain some bite.

◇ The amount of oil required for stir-frying may need to be increased slightly if you are using a frying pan (skillet) rather than a wok.

◇ If it appears that the contents of the pan are drying out or 'catching', do not add more oil at this stage as it will make the food greasy but add a little water instead.

◇ Follow either metric, imperial or American measures, and never be tempted to interchange.

◇ All spoon measurements are level: 1 tsp = 5 ml;
1 tbsp = 15 ml.

◇ Eggs are large.

◇ Always wash, peel and core, if necessary, fresh food before use.

◇ Use fresh herbs where possible. If you do use dried, use half the amount specified.

STARTERS

Woks are just made for cooking starters! Unusual starters can be conjured up in a wok from the most basic ingredients, which makes them ideal for impromptu entertaining. Experiment with stir-frying a simple selection of vegetables, then adding grated or cubed cheese at the last moment. Prawns (shrimp) and many types of shellfish can be stir-fried with a selection of your favourite spices, then finished of with a squeeze of lemon or lime juice or even a dash of cream for an exotic starter that's sure to impress.

All of these dishes can also be served as a light meal, and many can even be served as a main course with a crisp salad and some crusty bread.

PEARS WITH MELTING STILTON

—— SERVES 4 ——

	METRIC	IMPERIAL	AMERICAN
Groundnut (peanut) oil	10 ml	2 tsp	2 tsp
Small red onion, finely chopped	1	1	1
Firm, ripe pears, peeled, cored and cubed	4	4	4
Balsamic or red wine vinegar	15 ml	1 tbsp	1 tbsp
Stilton, diced	100 g	4 oz	1 cup
Salt and freshly ground black pepper			
A few endive (frisée lettuce) or curly lettuce leaves			

① Heat the wok or a large, deep frying pan (skillet).

② Pour the oil into the pan and when hot add the onion and stir-fry for about 1 minute or until the onion is transparent.

③ Add the pears and stir-fry for 1 minute.

④ Stir in the vinegar, then throw in the Stilton and turn briskly and briefly in the pan. Season to taste.

⑤ Arrange the lettuce leaves on individual plates and top with the pears and melting Stilton.

PREPARATION TIME: 5 MINUTES
COOKING TIME: 5 MINUTES

SUMMER CRAB STARTER

—— SERVES 4 ——

	METRIC	IMPERIAL	AMERICAN
Oil	15 ml	I tbsp	I tbsp
Shallot, finely chopped	I	I	I
Small leek, thinly sliced	I	I	I
White crabmeat	225 g	8 oz	8 oz
Lemon, juice and zest only	½	½	½
Crème fraîche	150 ml	¼ pt	⅔ cup
Salt and freshly ground black pepper			
For the topping:			
Oil	15 ml	I tbsp	I tbsp
Sliced white bread, crusts discarded, cut into I cm/½ in cubes	2	2	2
Chopped fresh dill (dill weed)	10 ml	2 tsp	2 tsp

① Heat the wok or a large heavy-based frying pan (skillet).

② Pour in the oil and when hot throw in the shallot and leek and stir-fry for 1–2 minutes until both are softened.

③ Gently stir in the crabmeat, lemon juice and zest and crème fraîche. Season to taste and heat through. Transfer the mixture to four ramekins (custard cups) and keep warm.

④ To make the topping, wipe out the wok or frying pan with kitchen paper (paper towels) and return it to the heat.

⑤ Add the oil to the pan and when very hot drop in the bread cubes and stir-fry for about 2 minutes or until lightly browned.

⑥ Mix the dill with the bread cubes, then sprinkle over the crab mixture in the ramekins.

PREPARATION TIME: 5 MINUTES
COOKING TIME: 8 MINUTES

MAPLE SYRUP AND HERB SHALLOTS

—— SERVES 4 ——

	METRIC	IMPERIAL	AMERICAN
Oil	30 ml	2 tbsp	2 tbsp
Small shallots, peeled and halved	350 g	12 oz	12 oz
A sprig of fresh thyme			
A sprig of fresh rosemary			
Salt	2.5 ml	½ tsp	½ tsp
Black pepper			
Maple syrup	30 ml	2 tbsp	2 tbsp
Vegetable stock	150 ml	¼ pt	⅔ cup
Honey-roast ham, diced	100 g	4 oz	1 cup

① Heat the wok or a large heavy-based frying pan (skillet).

② Pour the oil into the pan and when hot add the shallots and stir-fry for 3–6 minutes until they start to soften and turn translucent.

③ Add all the remaining ingredients except the ham. Stir well. Cover the pan, reduce the heat slightly and simmer for 10 minutes.

④ Remove the lid from the pan and stir in the ham.

⑤ Turn up the heat to full and boil for about 1 minute to reduce the amount of liquid slightly.

⑥ Serve hot.

PREPARATION TIME: 5 MINUTES
COOKING TIME: 18 MINUTES

CHINESE-STYLE SOUP

—— SERVES 4 ——

	METRIC	IMPERIAL	AMERICAN
Oil	15 ml	1 tbsp	1 tbsp
Garlic clove, crushed	1	1	1
Very finely chopped fresh root ginger	5 ml	1 tsp	1 tsp
Spring onions (scallions), very finely chopped	6	6	6
Red (bell) pepper, finely diced	½	½	½
Baby sweetcorn (corn), fresh or thawed frozen, finely sliced	4	4	4
Mangetout (snow peas), finely sliced	25 g	1 oz	1 oz
Dry sherry	30 ml	2 tbsp	2 tbsp
Soy sauce	25 ml	1½ tbsp	1½ tbsp
Brown sugar	10 ml	2 tsp	2 tsp
A pinch of Chinese five-spice powder			
Chicken or good vegetable stock	900 ml	1½ pts	3¾ cups

① Heat the wok or a large saucepan.

② Add the oil and when hot stir-fry the garlic, ginger and spring onions for about 1 minute.

③ Add the red pepper, sweetcorn and mangetout and cook for a further 1–2 minutes until the sweetcorn slices are slightly softened.

④ Stir in the remaining ingredients and bring the soup just to the boil, stirring occasionally.

⑤ Reduce the heat and simmer for 5 minutes. Serve hot.

PREPARATION TIME: 10 MINUTES
COOKING TIME: 10 MINUTES

ITALIAN STIR-FRY WITH MOZZARELLA

—— SERVES 4 ——

	METRIC	IMPERIAL	AMERICAN
Oil	15 ml	1 tbsp	1 tbsp
Garlic clove, crushed	1	1	1
Onion, sliced	1	1	1
Small red (bell) pepper, diced	½	½	½
Mushrooms, sliced	100 g	4 oz	4 oz
Ripe tomatoes, skinned and quartered	4	4	4
Chopped fresh oregano	15 ml	1 tbsp	1 tbsp
Tomato purée (paste)	15 ml	1 tbsp	1 tbsp
Black olives, pitted (stoned)	12	12	12
Mozzarella cheese, drained and diced	100 g	4 oz	1 cup

① Heat the wok or a large heavy-based frying pan (skillet).

② Pour the oil into the pan and when hot stir in the garlic and onion and cook for about 1 minute.

③ Stir in the red pepper, mushrooms and tomatoes and cook for about 2 minutes until the tomatoes have softened and started to break down.

④ Add the oregano, tomato purée and olives, stir well and cook for 1 minute.

⑤ Spoon the very hot mixture into warm bowls and sprinkle the Mozzarella over the top so that it starts to melt.

PREPARATION TIME: 15 MINUTES
COOKING TIME: 6 MINUTES

SPICED CHICKEN WITH PEACHES
—— SERVES 4 ——

	METRIC	IMPERIAL	AMERICAN
Oil	15 ml	1 tbsp	1 tbsp
Garlic clove, crushed	1	1	1
Small onion, finely chopped	1	1	1
Chicken breast meat, cut into thin strips	225 g	8 oz	8 oz
Canned peach halves, very finely chopped	4	4	4
Medium-hot curry paste	15 ml	1 tbsp	1 tbsp
Tomato purée (paste)	15 ml	1 tbsp	1 tbsp
Salt and freshly ground black pepper			
Sweet white wine	45 ml	3 tbsp	3 tbsp
Lemon juice	10 ml	2 tsp	2 tsp
Double (heavy) cream	150 ml	¼ pt	⅔ cup

① Heat the wok or a large heavy-based frying pan (skillet).

② Heat the oil, then add the garlic and onion and stir-fry for about 1 minute.

③ Add the chicken to the pan and stir-fry for 1–2 minutes or until it has changed colour.

④ Add the peaches, curry paste, tomato purée and salt and pepper and stir well.

⑤ Gradually blend in the wine and lemon juice.

⑥ Bring to the boil and cook for several minutes to reduce.

⑦ Stir in the cream and heat through without boiling.

PREPARATION TIME: 5 MINUTES
COOKING TIME: 8 MINUTES

SCALLOPS WITH SMOKED BACON

—— SERVES 4 ——

	METRIC	IMPERIAL	AMERICAN
Scallops, fresh or thawed frozen	12	12	12
Oil	15 ml	1 tbsp	1 tbsp
Small red onion, finely chopped	1	1	1
Thick smoked bacon, finely cubed	100 g	4 oz	4 oz
Lemon juice	5 ml	1 tsp	1 tsp
A few drops of Worcestershire sauce			
A pinch of salt			
A pinch of sugar			
Chopped fresh parsley	15 ml	1 tbsp	1 tbsp

① If using fresh scallops, detach them from their shells, wash them and then pat them dry. Cut each scallop into about four slices.

② Heat the wok or a large heavy-based frying pan (skillet).

③ Pour the oil into the pan and when hot add the onion and stir-fry for about 1 minute.

④ Add the bacon and cook for 1 minute.

⑤ Add the scallops and stir-fry until their edges start to curl.

⑥ Stir in the remaining ingredients and serve.

PREPARATION TIME: 10 MINUTES
COOKING TIME: 7 MINUTES

MUSHROOMS WITH WINE AND CREAM

—— SERVES 4 ——

	METRIC	IMPERIAL	AMERICAN
Oil	30 ml	2 tbsp	2 tbsp
Garlic clove, crushed	I	I	I
Shallot, finely chopped	I	I	I
Chestnut mushrooms, quartered	100 g	4 oz	4 oz
Flat dark-gilled mushrooms, thickly sliced	100 g	4 oz	4 oz
Shiitake mushrooms, halved	100 g	4 oz	4 oz
Oyster mushrooms, halved	100 g	4 oz	4 oz
White wine	45 ml	3 tbsp	3 tbsp
Double (heavy) cream	150 ml	¼ pt	⅔ cup
Salt and freshly ground black pepper			

① Heat the wok or a large heavy-based frying pan (skillet).

② Pour in the oil and when hot stir in the garlic and shallot and cook for about 1 minute.

③ Add the chestnut mushrooms to the pan and stir-fry for 1 minute.

④ Add the remaining mushrooms and stir-fry for about 2 minutes or until they start to soften.

⑤ Pour the wine into the pan and cook, stirring, until the amount of wine is slightly reduced.

⑥ Add the cream, season to taste, stir gently and heat through. Serve hot.

PREPARATION TIME: 10 MINUTES
COOKING TIME: 10 MINUTES

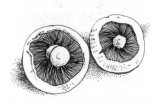

AUBERGINE AND ANCHOVY APPETISER
—— SERVES 4 ——

	METRIC	IMPERIAL	AMERICAN
Aubergines (eggplants)	450 g	I lb	I lb
Salt			
Oil	15 ml	I tbsp	I tbsp
Small onion, finely chopped	I	I	I
Garlic cloves, crushed	2	2	2
Ripe tomatoes, skinned and quartered	3	3	3
Tomato purée (paste)	10 ml	2 tsp	2 tsp
Canned anchovies, drained	50 g	2 oz	2 oz
A pinch of sugar			
Freshly ground black pepper			

① Cut the aubergines into 2.5 cm/1 in cubes, sprinkle with salt and leave for about 20 minutes.

② Rinse the aubergines in cold water, drain, then pat dry.

③ Heat the wok or a deep heavy-based frying pan (skillet). Add the oil and heat.

④ Add the onion and garlic and stir-fry until the onion is transparent.

⑤ Add the tomatoes and stir-fry for about 30 seconds until soft.

⑥ Stir in the remaining ingredients, adding a little water if the mixture seems too dry.

⑦ Cover the pan, reduce the heat and braise for about 3 minutes.

⑧ Stir, then serve hot in small individual bowls.

PREPARATION TIME: 30 MINUTES
COOKING TIME: 7 MINUTES

AVOCADOS WITH SHELLFISH
—— SERVES 4 ——

	METRIC	IMPERIAL	AMERICAN
Firm, ripe avocado pears	2	2	2
Oil	15 ml	1 tbsp	1 tbsp
Garlic clove, crushed	1	1	1
Mixed shellfish, e.g. mussels, prawns (shrimp), cockles, squid, fresh or thawed frozen	450 g	1 lb	1 lb
Salt and freshly ground black pepper			
Lemon juice	15 ml	1 tbsp	1 tbsp

1. Peel the avocados, remove the stones (pits) and cut the flesh into 2.5 cm/1 in cubes.

2. Heat the wok or a large heavy-based frying pan (skillet).

3. Add the oil and when it is hot add the garlic and stir-fry quickly and briefly.

4. Place the shellfish in the pan and stir-fry for 1–2 minutes.

5. Stir in the seasoning and lemon juice.

6. Mix in the avocado cubes, being careful not to break them up. Heat through and serve hot.

PREPARATION TIME: 5 MINUTES
COOKING TIME: 5 MINUTES

GREEN PEPPERED ONIONS

—— SERVES 4 ——

	METRIC	IMPERIAL	AMERICAN
Oil	15 ml	I tbsp	I tbsp
Large onions, sliced	2	2	2
Large red onions, sliced	2	2	2
Brown sugar	15 ml	I tbsp	I tbsp
Green peppercorns, roughly crushed	15 ml	I tbsp	I tbsp
A pinch of salt			
Thin French bread slices, lightly toasted	4	4	4

① Heat the wok or a large heavy-based frying pan (skillet).

② Pour in the oil and when it is hot add the onions and stir-fry for 1–2 minutes until softened.

③ Stir in the sugar, peppercorns and salt.

④ Spoon the onion mixture on to slices of French bread and serve hot.

PREPARATION TIME: 10 MINUTES
COOKING TIME: 5 MINUTES

SESAME MELBAS WITH PRAWNS
—— SERVES 4 ——

	METRIC	IMPERIAL	AMERICAN
Thick white bread slices	3	3	3
Egg, beaten	I	I	I
Sesame seeds	30 ml	2 tbsp	2 tbsp
Oil	45 ml	3 tbsp	3 tbsp
Cooked prawns (shrimp)	225 g	8 oz	8 oz
Lemon juice	30 ml	2 tbsp	2 tbsp

① Discard the crusts, then cut the bread into 2.5 cm/1 in cubes.

② Dip the cubes in the egg and then into the sesame seeds.

③ Heat the wok or a large heavy-based frying pan (skillet).

④ Pour in the oil and when it is hot add the bread cubes, a few at a time, and stir-fry until they are lightly browned all over.

⑤ Stir in the prawns carefully. Heat through for 30–60 seconds.

⑥ Serve in individual bowls with the lemon juice drizzled over the top.

PREPARATION TIME: 5 MINUTES
COOKING TIME: 5 MINUTES

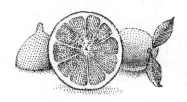

GINGERED BEANS IN BLACK BEAN SAUCE
—— SERVES 4 ——

	METRIC	IMPERIAL	AMERICAN
Oil	15 ml	1 tbsp	1 tbsp
Garlic clove, crushed	1	1	1
Finely chopped fresh root ginger	5 ml	1 tsp	1 tsp
Leek, finely sliced	1	1	1
Small red (bell) pepper, diced	½	½	½
Can of kidney beans, drained	430 g	15 oz	1 large
Can of borlotti beans, drained	430 g	15 oz	1 large
Black bean sauce	15 ml	1 tbsp	1 tbsp

1. Heat the wok or a large heavy-based frying pan (skillet).
2. Pour in the oil and when hot add the garlic and ginger and stir-fry for about 30 seconds.
3. Add the leek and red pepper to the pan and cook for 1–2 minutes until they lose their crispness.
4. Stir in all the beans and the black bean sauce.
5. Heat through and serve in individual bowls.

PREPARATION TIME: 5 MINUTES
COOKING TIME: 5 MINUTES

SEAFOOD DISHES

Seafood is the perfect wok food because it is at its best when cooked quickly to retain its texture and flavour, but it needs a gentle touch. Try cooking all types of fish in the wok, although the firmer varieties, such as cod and monkfish, and shellfish are best. As long as the fish is cut into thick strips and cooked for a minimal length of time, the resulting dish will be full of the tastes of the deep. Always ensure that the other flavours in the dish do not overpower the more delicate flavour of the fish.

Coating fish with flour, batter or breadcrumbs helps to protect it from the intense heat of the wok, but do not overcrowd the pan or you will end up with a big, soft mess. Instead, briskly but carefully cook a few pieces at a time, then remove them from the pan and keep warm while cooking the remainder.

SEAFOOD FRIED RICE

—— SERVES 4 ——

	METRIC	IMPERIAL	AMERICAN
Oil	30 ml	2 tbsp	2 tbsp
Garlic cloves, crushed	2	2	2
Onion, finely chopped	I	I	I
Leek, finely sliced	I	I	I
Mild green chilli, very finely chopped	I	I	I
Small red (bell) pepper, diced	I	I	I
Smoked bacon, finely chopped	25 g	I oz	I oz
Mixed shellfish, e.g. mussels prawns (shrimp), squid, fresh or thawed frozen	350 g	12 oz	12 oz
Cold cooked long-grain rice	450 g	I lb	4 cups
Salt	2.5 ml	½ tsp	½ tsp
Chopped fresh parsley	30 ml	2 tbsp	2 tbsp

① Heat the wok or a large heavy-based frying pan (skillet).

② Pour in the oil and when hot stir-fry the garlic, onion, leek and chilli for 1–2 minutes or until the leek and onion start to soften.

③ Add the pepper and bacon and cook for 1 minute.

④ Add the shellfish, rice and salt and stir thoroughly, ensuring that the mixture is hot all the way through.

⑤ Serve hot with the parsley sprinkled over.

PREPARATION TIME: 15 MINUTES
COOKING TIME: 7 MINUTES

CREAMY COD WITH BLUE CHEESE
—— SERVES 4 ——

	METRIC	IMPERIAL	AMERICAN
Oil	15 ml	I tbsp	I tbsp
Shallot, finely chopped	I	I	I
Celery, finely sliced	50 g	2 oz	2 oz
Mushrooms, sliced	100 g	4 oz	4 oz
Cod or other firm white fish fillet, cut into thick strips	450 g	I lb	I lb
Double (heavy) cream	45 ml	3 tbsp	3 tbsp
Soured (dairy sour) cream	45 ml	3 tbsp	3 tbsp
Blue cheese, crumbled	75 g	3 oz	¾ cup
Salt and freshly ground black pepper			

①   Heat the wok or a large heavy-based frying pan (skillet).

②   Pour in the oil and when hot add the shallot and celery and stir-fry for about 1 minute.

③   Add the mushrooms and fish to the pan and stir-fry carefully for 1 minute.

④   Pour in the creams and sprinkle in the cheese and cook, stirring, for 1–2 minutes so that the fish cooks and the cheese melts. Season to taste.

PREPARATION TIME: 10 MINUTES
COOKING TIME: 5 MINUTES

THAI-STYLE FISH WITH PRAWNS
—— SERVES 4 ——

	METRIC	IMPERIAL	AMERICAN
Oil	15 ml	1 tbsp	1 tbsp
Garlic cloves, crushed	3	3	3
Chopped fresh root ginger	10 ml	2 tsp	2 tsp
Chopped fresh lemon grass	15 ml	1 tbsp	1 tbsp
Shallots, finely chopped	2	2	2
Chilli powder	5 ml	1 tsp	1 tsp
Firm white fish fillet, cut into thick strips	450 g	1 lb	1 lb
Canned coconut milk	300 ml	½ pt	1¼ cups
Salt	2.5 ml	½ tsp	½ tsp
Thai fish sauce	10 ml	2 tsp	2 tsp
Lime juice	10 ml	2 tsp	2 tsp
Cooked prawns (shrimp)	100 g	4 oz	4 oz
Chopped fresh coriander (cilantro)	10 ml	2 tsp	2 tsp

1. Heat the wok or a large heavy-based frying pan (skillet).
2. Pour in the oil and when hot add the garlic, ginger, lemon grass and shallots and stir-fry for about 1 minute.
3. Stir in the chilli powder, then carefully add the fish and stir-fry for about 1 minute.
4. Gently stir in the coconut milk, salt, fish sauce and lime juice and cook, stirring, for 1–2 minutes.
5. Finally, stir in the prawns and serve garnished with the chopped coriander.

Serving suggestion: Serve hot with rice.

PREPARATION TIME: 15 MINUTES
COOKING TIME: 7 MINUTES

CHILLI STIR-FRIED SQUID

—— SERVES 4 ——

	METRIC	IMPERIAL	AMERICAN
Oil	30 ml	2 tbsp	2 tbsp
Garlic cloves, crushed	2	2	2
Chopped fresh root ginger	10 ml	2 tsp	2 tsp
Small fresh red chilli, finely chopped	1	1	1
Fresh mild green chilli, very finely chopped	1	1	1
Spring onions (scallions)	5	5	5
Yellow (bell) pepper, diced	½	½	½
Cornflour (cornstarch)	5 ml	1 tsp	1 tsp
Water	60 ml	4 tbsp	4 tbsp
Dry sherry	30 ml	2 tbsp	2 tbsp
Soy sauce	30 ml	2 tbsp	2 tbsp
Oyster sauce	10 ml	2 tsp	2 tsp
Squid, fresh or thawed frozen, cut into rings	450 g	1 lb	1 lb

① Heat the wok or a large heavy-based frying pan (skillet).

② Pour in the oil and when very hot add the garlic, ginger and chillies and stir-fry for about 2 minutes.

③ Add the spring onions and yellow pepper and stir-fry for 1 minute.

④ Blend the cornflour with the water and add this to the pan with the sherry, sauces and squid.

⑤ Cook for about 1 minute, stirring constantly, or until the sauce has thickened and the squid has turned white.

Serving suggestion: Serve hot with rice or pasta.

PREPARATION TIME: 10 MINUTES
COOKING TIME: 7 MINUTES

HADDOCK IN SPINACH AND HERBS
—— SERVES 4 ——

	METRIC	IMPERIAL	AMERICAN
Oil	30 ml	2 tbsp	2 tbsp
Haddock, or other firm white fish fillet, cut into thick strips	450 g	1 lb	1 lb
Garlic clove, crushed	1	1	1
Leeks, finely sliced	2	2	2
Chopped fresh dill (dill weed)	15 ml	1 tbsp	1 tbsp
Chopped fresh parsley	30 ml	2 tbsp	2 tbsp
Fresh spinach, finely shredded	100 g	4 oz	4 oz
A pinch of grated nutmeg			
White wine	60 ml	4 tbsp	4 tbsp
Crème fraîche	30 ml	2 tbsp	2 tbsp
Salt and freshly ground black pepper			

① Heat the wok or a large heavy-based frying pan (skillet).

② Pour in the oil and when very hot add the fish and stir-fry gently for about 1–2 minutes, being careful not to break it up.

③ Lift the fish out of the pan with a draining spoon and transfer to a plate. Keep warm.

④ Reheat the pan and add the garlic, leeks, chopped herbs, spinach and nutmeg. Stir-fry for about 2–3 minutes or until the leeks are quite soft.

⑤ Add the wine to the pan and bring it to the boil, stirring. Cook for several minutes to reduce the amount of wine slightly.

⑥ Stir in the crème fraîche, then return the fish to the pan. Season to taste and heat through.

Serving suggestion: Serve hot with creamed potatoes and a selection of hot vegetables.

PREPARATION TIME: 15 MINUTES
COOKING TIME: 10 MINUTES

CREAMY CUCUMBER COD

—— SERVES 4 ——

	METRIC	IMPERIAL	AMERICAN
Oil	15 ml	1 tbsp	1 tbsp
Small shallot, finely chopped	1	1	1
Cod fillets, cut into 2.5 cm/1 in wide strips	450 g	1 lb	1 lb
Cucumber, peeled, seeded and very finely chopped	100 g	4 oz	4 oz
Greek-style natural yoghurt	30 ml	2 tbsp	2 tbsp
Double (heavy) cream	30 ml	2 tbsp	2 tbsp
A pinch of sugar			
Salt and freshly ground black pepper			

1. Heat the wok or a large heavy-based frying pan (skillet).

2. Pour in the oil and when hot add the shallot and stir-fry for about 1 minute until it has softened.

3. Carefully add the fish to the pan and stir-fry for about 2 minutes.

4. Add the cucumber and, still being careful not to break up the fish, cook for 1–2 minutes, ensuring that some of the water it gives off evaporates.

5. Gently stir in the remaining ingredients and heat through.

Serving suggestion: Serve hot with a selection of seasonable vegetables.

PREPARATION TIME: 10 MINUTES
COOKING TIME: 8 MINUTES

ORANGE BASS
—— SERVES 4 ——

	METRIC	IMPERIAL	AMERICAN
Oil	15 ml	1 tbsp	1 tbsp
Onion, finely chopped	1	1	1
Celery, finely sliced	100 g	4 oz	4 oz
Bass, skinned, boned and cut into chunks	350 g	12 oz	12 oz
Cornflour (cornstarch)	5 ml	1 tsp	1 tsp
Water	30 ml	2 tbsp	2 tbsp
Fresh orange juice	30 ml	2 tbsp	2 tbsp
Grated orange zest	10 ml	2 tsp	2 tsp
Salt and freshly ground black pepper			
A pinch of sugar			

① Heat the wok or a large heavy-based frying pan (skillet).

② Pour in the oil and when it is hot add the onion and celery and stir-fry for about 2 minutes or until both have softened slightly.

③ Add the bass to the pan and stir very carefully for about 1 minute.

④ Blend the cornflour with the water and add to the fish mixture with the orange juice and zest, seasoning and sugar.

⑤ Stir gently until the sauce has thickened slightly.

Serving suggestion: Serve hot with green vegetables and boiled new potatoes.

PREPARATION TIME: 15 MINUTES
COOKING TIME: 6 MINUTES

COD WITH PASTA IN TOMATO SAUCE

—— SERVES 4 ——

	METRIC	IMPERIAL	AMERICAN
Oil	15 ml	1 tbsp	1 tbsp
Garlic cloves, crushed	2	2	2
Large onion, chopped	1	1	1
Medium red (bell) pepper, diced	1	1	1
Ripe tomatoes, skinned and chopped	4	4	4
Red wine	30 ml	2 tbsp	2 tbsp
Cod fillets, skinned, boned and cut into thick strips	350 g	12 oz	12 oz
Tomato purée (paste)	15 ml	1 tbsp	1 tbsp
Chopped fresh oregano	10 ml	2 tsp	2 tsp
Chopped fresh basil	5 ml	1 tsp	1 tsp
Precooked pasta shapes	75 g	3 oz	3 oz

①　Heat the wok or a large, deep heavy-based frying pan (skillet).

②　Pour in the oil and when hot add the garlic and onion and stir-fry for about 1 minute.

③　Add the red pepper and cook for 1 minute.

④　Stir in the tomatoes and wine and cook for 2–3 minutes.

⑤　Carefully stir in the remaining ingredients and cook for several minutes to cook the fish and ensure that the pasta is hot.

Serving suggestion: Serve hot with garlic bread.

PREPARATION TIME: 5 MINUTES
COOKING TIME: 15 MINUTES

THAI-STYLE SALMON
—— SERVES 4 ——

	METRIC	IMPERIAL	AMERICAN
Oil	15 ml	1 tbsp	1 tbsp
Garlic clove, crushed	1	1	1
Chopped fresh root ginger	5 ml	1 tsp	1 tsp
Finely chopped lemon grass	15 ml	1 tbsp	1 tbsp
Salmon fillet, cut into thick strips	350 g	12 oz	12 oz
Finely chopped fresh chives	30 ml	2 tbsp	2 tbsp
Lime juice	15 ml	1 tbsp	1 tbsp

① Heat the wok or a large heavy-based frying pan (skillet).

② Pour in the oil and when hot add the garlic and ginger and stir-fry for 30 seconds.

③ Add the lemon grass and cook for 30 seconds.

④ Carefully add the salmon to the pan and gently stir-fry for about 1 minute only or the fish will break up.

⑤ Gently stir in the chives and serve with the lime juice drizzled over the top.

Serving suggestion: Serve hot with boiled rice.

PREPARATION TIME: 10 MINUTES

COOKING TIME: 4 MINUTES

MONKFISH AND COCKLES IN GARLIC CREAM

—— SERVES 4 ——

	METRIC	IMPERIAL	AMERICAN
Oil	15 ml	1 tbsp	1 tbsp
Garlic cloves, finely chopped	2	2	2
Onion, finely chopped	1	1	1
Monkfish, cut into chunks	225 g	8 oz	8 oz
Sweet vermouth	60 ml	4 tbsp	4 tbsp
Cockles	225 g	8 oz	8 oz
Double (heavy) cream	150 ml	¼ pt	⅔ cup
Salt and freshly ground black pepper			

① Heat the wok or a large heavy-based frying pan (skillet). Pour in the oil and heat.

② Add the garlic and onion and stir-fry for about 1 minute.

③ Add the monkfish to the pan and stir carefully for about 2 minutes.

④ Pour in the vermouth. Stir and cook the mixture for 2–3 minutes until the vermouth is reduced by half.

⑤ Stir in the cockles and cream and heat through. Season well.

Serving suggestion: Serve hot with creamed potatoes and hot vegetables.

PREPARATION TIME: 10 MINUTES
COOKING TIME: 9 MINUTES

PRAWNS WITH AVOCADO CREAM SAUCE
—— SERVES 4 ——

	METRIC	IMPERIAL	AMERICAN
Uncooked prawns (shrimp)	450 g	I lb	I lb
Avocado pear, peeled, stoned (pitted) and mashed	I	I	I
Lime juice	10 ml	2 tsp	2 tsp
Garlic cloves, crushed	2	2	2
Tomato purée (paste)	5 ml	I tsp	I tsp
Soured (dairy sour) cream	150 ml	¼ pt	⅔ cup
A pinch of cayenne pepper			
A pinch of salt			
Oil	15 ml	I tbsp	I tbsp
Spring onions (scallions), chopped	3	3	3
Chopped fresh parsley	10 ml	2 tsp	2 tsp

① Peel and de-vein the prawns, then wash and dry.

② Combine the mashed avocado with the lime juice, one of the garlic cloves, the tomato purée, soured cream, cayenne pepper and salt. Mix well to give a smooth sauce.

③ Heat the wok or a large heavy-based frying pan (skillet).

④ Pour in the oil and when hot stir-fry the remaining garlic and the spring onions for about 30 seconds.

⑤ Add the prawns and cook for 1 minute.

⑥ Stir in the avocado sauce and cook, stirring, for about 2–3 minutes until the sauce is heated through but not boiling.

⑦ Serve hot, sprinkled with the parsley.

Serving suggestion: Serve with boiled new potatoes.

PREPARATION TIME: 25 MINUTES
COOKING TIME: 7 MINUTES

MONKFISH WITH ALMONDS

—— SERVES 4 ——

	METRIC	IMPERIAL	AMERICAN
Monkfish	450 g	I lb	I lb
Oil	30 ml	2 tbsp	2 tbsp
Garlic clove, crushed	I	I	I
Parboiled new potatoes, sliced	175 g	6 oz	6 oz
Blanched whole almonds	75 g	3 oz	¾ cup
Salt and freshly ground black pepper			
Chopped fresh dill (dill weed)	5 ml	I tsp	I tsp

①   Cut the monkfish into fairly thick strips 5 cm/2 in long.

②   Heat the wok or a large heavy-based frying pan (skillet).

③   Pour in the oil and when hot stir-fry the garlic for about 30 seconds.

④   Add the potatoes and almonds to the pan and cook, stirring, for about 1–2 minutes until the potatoes are golden at the edges.

⑤   Carefully add the monkfish and stir-fry gently for about 2 minutes, avoiding breaking up the flesh.

⑥   Finally, sprinkle on plenty of salt and pepper and the dill and stir once more before serving.

Serving suggestion: Serve piping hot with a crisp side salad.

PREPARATION TIME: 10 MINUTES
COOKING TIME: 6 MINUTES

LEMON FISH WITH MANGETOUT
—— SERVES 4 ——

	METRIC	IMPERIAL	AMERICAN
Cod	225 g	8 oz	8 oz
Salmon	225 g	8 oz	8 oz
Oil	30 ml	2 tbsp	2 tbsp
Mangetout (snow peas), trimmed	100 g	4 oz	4 oz
Lemon, grated rind and juice only	1	1	1
Salt and freshly ground black pepper			

① Skin and bone the cod and the salmon and cut into thick strips.

② Heat the wok or a large heavy-based frying pan (skillet).

③ Add the oil and when hot add the fish and mangetout, stirring gently to prevent the fish from breaking up. Cook for 1–2 minutes.

④ Stir through the lemon rind and juice. Season to taste.

Serving suggestion: Serve hot with new potatoes and a crisp green salad.

PREPARATION TIME: 10 MINUTES
COOKING TIME: 5 MINUTES

SEAFOOD CHOW MEIN
—— SERVES 4 ——

	METRIC	IMPERIAL	AMERICAN
Dried egg noodles	225 g	8 oz	8 oz
Oil	15 ml	1 tbsp	1 tbsp
Garlic cloves, crushed	2	2	2
Spring onions (scallions), finely sliced	4	4	4
Mangetout (snow peas), trimmed	75 g	3 oz	3 oz
Cod fillets, fresh or thawed frozen, cut into thick strips	225 g	8 oz	8 oz
Soy sauce	10 ml	2 tsp	2 tsp
Sugar	5 ml	1 tsp	1 tsp
Vinegar	5 ml	1 tsp	1 tsp
Sesame oil	5 ml	1 tsp	1 tsp
Cooked prawns (shrimp)	100 g	4 oz	1 cup

① Cook the noodles according to the packet instructions and drain.

② Heat the wok or a large heavy-based frying pan (skillet).

③ Pour in the oil and when hot add the garlic, onion and mangetout and stir-fry for about 1 minute.

④ Add the fish to the pan and carefully stir-fry for 1 minute.

⑤ Stir in the noodles and all the remaining ingredients and continue to stir-fry for 2–3 minutes until the mixture is hot right through.

Serving suggestion: Serve with a crisp green salad.

PREPARATION TIME: 10 MINUTES
COOKING TIME: 6 MINUTES

COD WITH SMOKED MUSSELS

—— SERVES 4 ——

	METRIC	IMPERIAL	AMERICAN
Oil	15 ml	1 tbsp	1 tbsp
Garlic cloves, crushed	2	2	2
Onion, chopped	1	1	1
Cod fillets, cut into 2.5 cm/1 in cubes	450 g	1 lb	1 lb
Large ripe tomatoes, skinned and chopped	4	4	4
Tomato purée (paste)	30 ml	2 tbsp	2 tbsp
Chopped fresh basil	30 ml	2 tbsp	2 tbsp
Fish or vegetable stock	150 ml	¼ pt	⅔ cup
Can of smoked mussels, drained	85 g	3½ oz	1 small

① Heat the wok or a large heavy-based frying pan (skillet).

② Pour in the oil and when hot stir-fry the garlic and onion for 1 minute.

③ Add the fish to the pan and stir-fry carefully for about 1 minute.

④ Gently stir in the remaining ingredients and cook, stirring, for 3–4 minutes until the tomatoes are soft and pulpy.

Serving suggestion: Serve hot with buttered tagliatelle.

PREPARATION TIME: 10 MINUTES
COOKING TIME: 7 MINUTES

SWEET FENNEL MONKFISH
—— SERVES 4 ——

	METRIC	IMPERIAL	AMERICAN
Monkfish	450 g	1 lb	1 lb
Oil	15 ml	1 tbsp	1 tbsp
Shallots, finely sliced	2	2	2
Fennel heads, trimmed and green fronds reserved	3	3	3
Sweet cider	60 ml	4 tbsp	4 tbsp
Brown sugar	10 ml	2 tsp	2 tsp
Green peppercorns, crushed	5 ml	1 tsp	1 tsp
A pinch of salt			

① Skin and bone the monkfish and cut the flesh into thick strips.

② Heat the wok or a large heavy-based frying pan (skillet).

③ Pour in the oil and heat, then add the shallots and the fennel and stir-fry for about 4–5 minutes until the fennel is tender.

④ Add the monkfish to the pan and cook, stirring carefully, for about 1 minute.

⑤ Add the remaining ingredients and continue to cook for 2–3 minutes until fish is cooked but not breaking up.

⑥ Serve hot, garnished with the fennel fronds.

Serving suggestion: Serve with boiled new potatoes.

PREPARATION TIME: 10 MINUTES
COOKING TIME: 10 MINUTES

CRUNCHY CRAB WITH CHINESE LEAVES

—— SERVES 4 ——

	METRIC	IMPERIAL	AMERICAN
Oil	15 ml	1 tbsp	1 tbsp
French (green) beans, trimmed and cut into short lengths	50 g	2 oz	2 oz
Spring onions (scallions), chopped	5	5	5
Chinese leaves, finely shredded	100 g	4 oz	4 oz
Canned water chestnuts, drained and sliced	50 g	2 oz	2 oz
Cashew nuts	50 g	2 oz	½ cup
Fresh crabmeat	350 g	12 oz	12 oz
Soy sauce	15 ml	1 tbsp	1 tbsp
Oyster sauce	15 ml	1 tbsp	1 tbsp
Dry sherry	15 ml	1 tbsp	1 tbsp
Sugar	5 ml	1 tsp	1 tsp
Cashew nuts, to garnish			

①   Heat the wok or a large heavy-based frying pan (skillet).

②   Pour in the oil and when hot add the beans, spring onions, Chinese leaves, water chestnuts and the measured cashew nuts and stir-fry for about 2 minutes.

③   Stir in the remaining ingredients and heat through.

④   Serve hot, sprinkled with a few cashew nuts.

Serving suggestion: Serve with egg noodles.

PREPARATION TIME: 10 MINUTES
COOKING TIME: 6 MINUTES

MEAT DISHES

Most meat lends itself very well to stir-frying, provided it is either a tender cut or has already been tenderised. Marinades not only tenderise but also introduce extra flavours to the dish. A simple marinade can be a little vinegar and sugar but try different mixtures of an acidic ingredient with spices or seasonings. Don't be tempted to use only expensive cuts of meat: quite often they have less flavour than slightly tougher and cheaper cuts. Most recipes here recommend cutting the meat into thin strips so it cooks efficiently and retains its flavour and texture.

Stir-fried meat can be spicy, saucy, cheesy, crispy ... the variations are endless! Be daring and introduce flavours from all over the world and accompany the dish with pasta, rice or potatoes or just fresh crusty bread.

MARINER'S BEEF
—— SERVES 4 ——

	METRIC	IMPERIAL	AMERICAN
Oil	15 ml	1 tbsp	1 tbsp
Garlic clove, crushed	1	1	1
Spring onions (scallions), chopped	4	4	4
Beef, cut into thin strips	350 g	12 oz	12 oz
Cooked prawns (shrimp)	100 g	4 oz	4 oz
Scallops, fresh or thawed frozen, each cut into 4 slices	6	6	6
Salt and freshly ground black pepper			
Lemon juice	15 ml	1 tbsp	1 tbsp
Chopped fresh parsley	15 ml	1 tbsp	1 tbsp

① Heat the wok or a large heavy-based frying pan (skillet).

② Pour in the oil and when hot stir-fry the garlic and spring onions for about 30 seconds.

③ Add the beef to the pan and cook for 3–4 minutes or until it is tender.

④ Stir in the prawns and scallop slices and cook for 1 minute.

⑤ Season to taste and stir in the lemon juice and parsley.

Serving suggestion: Serve hot with noodles.

PREPARATION TIME: 15 MINUTES
COOKING TIME: 8 MINUTES

BEEF WITH WHISKY AND MUSTARD
—— SERVES 4 ——

	METRIC	IMPERIAL	AMERICAN
Oil	30 ml	2 tbsp	2 tbsp
Large onion, sliced	1	1	1
Large carrot, very finely sliced	1	1	1
Celery sticks, finely sliced	2	2	2
Lean beef, cut into fine strips	450 g	1 lb	1 lb
Dried mixed herbs	2.5 ml	½ tsp	½ tsp
Wholegrain mustard	15 ml	1 tbsp	1 tbsp
Brown sugar	15 ml	1 tbsp	1 tbsp
Whisky	30 ml	2 tbsp	2 tbsp
Beef stock	300 ml	½ pt	1¼ cups
Cornflour (cornstarch)	10 ml	2 tsp	2 tsp

1. Heat the wok or a large heavy-based frying pan (skillet).

2. Pour in the oil and when hot add the onion, carrot and celery and stir-fry for about 2 minutes until slightly softened.

3. Add the beef and herbs and cook for 3 minutes or until tender.

4. Stir in the mustard, sugar, whisky and stock.

5. Cover the pan, reduce the heat and simmer for 5 minutes.

6. Blend the cornflour with a little water and stir into the pan.

7. Increase the heat and cook, stirring, until the gravy is slightly thickened.

Serving suggestion: Serve hot with warm bread.

PREPARATION TIME: 10 MINUTES
COOKING TIME: 15 MINUTES

KASHMIRI-STYLE LAMB

—— SERVES 4 ——

	METRIC	IMPERIAL	AMERICAN
Oil	30 ml	2 tbsp	2 tbsp
Cumin seeds	5 ml	I tsp	I tsp
Cardamom pods, lightly crushed	4	4	4
Cloves, crushed	4	4	4
Onions, sliced	2	2	2
Garlic cloves, crushed	2	2	2
Chopped fresh root ginger	15 ml	I tbsp	I tbsp
Lean lamb, cut into fine strips	450 g	I lb	I lb
Chilli powder	5 ml	I tsp	I tsp
Ground cinnamon	5 ml	I tsp	I tsp
Medium-hot curry powder	5 ml	I tsp	I tsp
Salt	2.5 ml	½ tsp	½ tsp
Natural yoghurt	150 ml	¼ pt	⅔ cup

① Heat the wok or a large heavy-based frying pan (skillet).

② Add the oil, heat and then add the cumin seeds, cardamom and cloves and stir-fry for 30 seconds.

③ Add the onion, garlic and ginger and stir-fry until softened.

④ Add the lamb and stir-fry for about 3 minutes until it has changed colour.

⑤ Stir in the chilli powder, cinnamon, curry powder and salt.

⑥ Pour in the yoghurt, stir and heat through.

Serving suggestion: Serve hot with pilau rice.

PREPARATION TIME: 15 MINUTES
COOKING TIME: 10 MINUTES

LAMB WITH APRICOTS AND ALMONDS

—— SERVES 4 ——

	METRIC	IMPERIAL	AMERICAN
Boneless lamb, cut into fine strips	450 g	I lb	I lb
Plain (all-purpose) flour, seasoned	30 ml	2 tbsp	2 tbsp
Oil	30 ml	2 tbsp	2 tbsp
Shallot, finely chopped	I	I	I
Can of apricot halves, drained	410 g	14½ oz	I large
Salt and freshly ground black pepper			
Flaked almonds, lightly toasted	25 g	I oz	¼ cup

1. Coat the pieces of lamb in the seasoned flour.
2. Heat the wok or a large heavy-based frying pan (skillet).
3. Pour in the oil and when hot add the shallot and cook for about 30 seconds.
4. Add the lamb to the pan and stir-fry for 4–5 minutes until it is tender and a little crisp.
5. Stir in the apricot halves and season to taste, then cook for several minutes until it is heated through.
6. Serve with the toasted almonds sprinkled over the surface.

Serving suggestion: Serve hot with a crisp salad.

PREPARATION TIME: 5 MINUTES
COOKING TIME: 9 MINUTES

ROSEMARY LAMB
—— SERVES 4 ——

	METRIC	IMPERIAL	AMERICAN
Oil	30 ml	2 tbsp	2 tbsp
Garlic clove, crushed	I	I	I
Large red onion, roughly sliced	I	I	I
Chopped fresh rosemary	10 ml	2 tsp	2 tsp
Boneless lamb, cut into fine strips	450 g	I lb	I lb
Redcurrant jelly (clear conserve)	30 ml	2 tbsp	2 tbsp
Stock	45 ml	3 tbsp	3 tbsp
Red wine	30 ml	2 tbsp	2 tbsp
Salt and freshly ground black pepper			
Fresh rosemary sprigs	4	4	4

① Heat the wok or a large heavy-based frying pan (skillet).

② Pour in the oil and when hot add the garlic and onion and cook for 1 minute

③ Stir in the chopped rosemary and the lamb and cook for about 3–4 minutes or until the meat is tender.

④ Add the jelly, stock and wine. Season to taste and cook for about 2 minutes.

⑤ Serve garnished with the rosemary sprigs.

Serving suggestion: Serve hot with French fries.

PREPARATION TIME: 10 MINUTES
COOKING TIME: 9 MINUTES

LAMB WITH BABY VEGETABLES
—— SERVES 4 ——

	METRIC	IMPERIAL	AMERICAN
Baby carrots, scrubbed, topped and tailed	100 g	4 oz	4 oz
Baby new potatoes, scrubbed	100 g	4 oz	4 oz
Baby courgettes (zucchini), trimmed	100 g	4 oz	4 oz
Oil	30 ml	2 tbsp	2 tbsp
Baby shallots, halved	8	8	8
Minced (ground) lamb	450 g	I lb	I lb
Mint jelly (clear conserve)	30 ml	2 tbsp	2 tbsp
Lamb or beef stock	150 ml	¼ pt	⅔ cup
Frozen peas	50 g	2 oz	2 oz
Salt and freshly ground black pepper			
Fresh mint sprigs	4	4	4

① Bring a saucepan of water to the boil, then put in the carrots and potatoes and cook for about 3 minutes.

② Add the courgettes to the boiling water and cook for a further 2 minutes. Drain the vegetables well.

③ Heat the wok or a large heavy-based frying pan (skillet).

④ Pour in the oil and when hot add the shallots and stir-fry for about 3 minutes or until they start to soften.

⑤ Add the lamb to the pan and cook for 3–4 minutes or until well browned.

⑥ Add the baby vegetables to the pan and stir. Cook for 2 minutes.

⑦ Finally, stir in the mint jelly, stock and peas, then season to taste and heat through. Garnish with the mint sprigs.

Serving suggestion: Serve hot with boiled new potatoes.

PREPARATION TIME: 10 MINUTES
COOKING TIME: 18 MINUTES

LAMBS' LIVER WITH BARBECUE SAUCE

—— SERVES 4 ——

	METRIC	IMPERIAL	AMERICAN
Oil	15 ml	1 tbsp	1 tbsp
Garlic cloves, crushed	2	2	2
Onion, finely chopped	1	1	1
Small red (bell) pepper, cut into thin strips	1	1	1
Lambs' liver, cut into thin strips	350 g	12 oz	12 oz
Tomato purée (paste)	5 ml	1 tsp	1 tsp
Vinegar	30 ml	2 tbsp	2 tbsp
Brown sugar	15 ml	1 tbsp	1 tbsp
Honey	15 ml	1 tbsp	1 tbsp
Mustard powder	5 ml	1 tsp	1 tsp
Chilli powder	2.5 ml	½ tsp	½ tsp
Water	150 ml	¼ pt	⅔ cup

① Heat the wok or a large heavy-based frying pan (skillet).

② Pour in the oil and when hot add the garlic and stir-fry for 30 seconds.

③ Add the onion and pepper and cook for 1 minute.

④ Add the liver to the pan and fry (sauté) for about 3 minutes or until the juices are no longer bloody.

⑤ Stir in all the remaining ingredients and cook, stirring, for a further 3 minutes.

Serving suggestion: Serve hot with boiled rice.

PREPARATION TIME: 10 MINUTES
COOKING TIME: 9 MINUTES

KIDNEYS IN SHERRY AND REDCURRANT
—— SERVES 4 ——

	METRIC	IMPERIAL	AMERICAN
Lambs' kidneys	12	12	12
Plain (all-purpose) flour	30 ml	2 tbsp	2 tbsp
Oil	15 ml	1 tbsp	1 tbsp
Small onion, chopped	1	1	1
Button mushrooms, quartered	50 g	2 oz	2 oz
Beef stock	300 ml	½ pt	1¼ cups
Sweet sherry	60 ml	4 tbsp	4 tbsp
Redcurrant jelly (clear conserve)	15 ml	1 tbsp	1 tbsp
Salt and freshly ground black pepper			

1. Skin and core the kidneys and cut each into four pieces. Coat each piece with the flour.
2. Heat a wok or large heavy-based frying pan (skillet).
3. Pour in the oil and when hot cook the onion for 1 minute.
4. Add the kidneys and mushrooms and stir-fry for 3–4 minutes or until the juices run clear.
5. Stir in any remaining flour, then gradually blend in the stock and sherry. Cook, stirring, for several minutes so that the sherry sauce thickens slightly.
6. Stir in the redcurrant jelly until it is dissolved. Season to taste.

Serving suggestion: Serve hot with buttered noodles.

PREPARATION TIME: 15 MINUTES
COOKING TIME: 10 MINUTES

PORK IN PEANUT SAUCE
—— SERVES 4 ——

	METRIC	IMPERIAL	AMERICAN
Lean pork, cut into very fine strips	225 g	8 oz	8 oz
Soy sauce	15 ml	1 tbsp	1 tbsp
Vinegar	15 ml	1 tbsp	1 tbsp
Sugar	5 ml	1 tsp	1 tsp
Chinese five-spice powder	2.5 ml	½ tsp	½ tsp
Garlic cloves, crushed	2	2	2
Oil	30 ml	2 tbsp	2 tbsp
Onion, finely sliced	1	1	1
Carrot, cut into fine sticks	1	1	1
Large stick of celery, finely sliced	1	1	1
French (green) beans, cut into short lengths	25 g	1 oz	1 oz
Peanut butter	30 ml	2 tbsp	2 tbsp
Cornflour (cornstarch)	5 ml	1 tsp	1 tsp
Water	45 ml	3 tbsp	3 tbsp
Salted peanuts, roughly crushed	30 ml	2 tbsp	2 tbsp

① Combine the pork with the soy sauce, vinegar, sugar, spice and garlic and leave for about 10 minutes.

② Heat the wok or a large heavy-based frying pan (skillet).

③ Add the oil and when hot drop in the strips of pork reserving the marinade. Stir for a few minutes.

④ Add the onion, carrot, celery and beans and stir-fry until the meat is cooked and the vegetables slightly softened.

⑤ Mix in the marinade and the peanut butter.

⑥ Blend the cornflour with the water, then stir into the wok and continue to cook until the sauce has thickened.

⑦ Sprinkle the peanuts over the top.

Serving suggestion: Serve hot with boiled rice.

PREPARATION TIME: 10 MINUTES PLUS MARINATING
COOKING TIME: 10 MINUTES

PORK WITH SPINACH
—— SERVES 4 ——

	METRIC	IMPERIAL	AMERICAN
Oil	30 ml	2 tbsp	2 tbsp
Garlic clove, crushed	I	I	I
Small onion, finely chopped	I	I	I
Boneless pork, cut into fine strips	450 g	I lb	I lb
Fresh spinach, finely chopped	350 g	12 oz	12 oz
A pinch of grated nutmeg			
Salt and freshly ground black pepper			
Soured (dairy sour) cream	150 ml	¼ pt	⅔ cup
Pine kernels, lightly toasted	25 g	I oz	¼ cup

① Heat the wok or a large heavy-based frying pan (skillet).

② Pour in the oil and when hot add the garlic and onion and cook for about 30 seconds.

③ Add the pork and stir-fry for 3–4 minutes or until the meat is tender.

④ Stir in the spinach and cook for 30–60 seconds until it is wilted.

⑤ Add the nutmeg, season to taste, then stir in the cream. Heat through.

⑥ Serve garnished with the toasted pine kernels.

Serving suggestion: Serve hot with a crisp salad.

PREPARATION TIME: 15 MINUTES
COOKING TIME: 8 MINUTES

CHINESE-STYLE PORK WITH MANGETOUT

—— SERVES 4 ——

	METRIC	IMPERIAL	AMERICAN
Oil	30 ml	2 tbsp	2 tbsp
Garlic clove, crushed	1	1	1
Chopped fresh root ginger	10 ml	2 tsp	2 tsp
Mild fresh green chilli, finely diced	1	1	1
Baby new carrots, halved lengthways	6	6	6
Spring onions (scallions), cut into short lengths	4	4	4
Mangetout (snow peas), trimmed	50 g	2 oz	2 oz
Baby sweetcorn (corn), fresh or thawed frozen	8	8	8
Boneless pork, cut into fine strips	350 g	12 oz	12 oz
Beansprouts	50 g	2 oz	2 oz
Sweet chilli sauce	15 ml	1 tbsp	1 tbsp
Soy sauce	10 ml	2 tsp	2 tsp
Vinegar	5 ml	1 tsp	1 tsp
A pinch of sugar			

① Heat the wok or a large heavy-based frying pan (skillet).

② Pour in the oil and when hot add the garlic, ginger and chilli and stir-fry for 30 seconds.

③ Add the carrots and stir-fry for 1–2 minutes until slightly softened.

④ Add the onions, mangetout and sweetcorn and cook for 30 seconds.

⑤ Stir in the pork and cook for 3–4 minutes or until tender.

⑥ Carefully stir in the beansprouts and all the remaining ingredients and heat through.

Serving suggestion: Serve hot with boiled rice

PREPARATION TIME: 15 MINUTES
COOKING TIME: 10 MINUTES

CIDER AND APPLE PORK

—— SERVES 4 ——

	METRIC	IMPERIAL	AMERICAN
Oil	15 ml	I tbsp	I tbsp
Large onion, finely chopped	I	I	I
Garlic clove, crushed	I	I	I
Minced (ground) pork	450 g	I lb	I lb
Mushrooms, quartered	100 g	4 oz	4 oz
Large eating (dessert) apple, peeled, cored and cubed	I	I	I
Medium-dry cider	150 ml	¼ pt	⅔ cup
Apple chutney	30 ml	2 tbsp	2 tbsp
Ground mace	2.5 ml	½ tsp	½ tsp
Salt and freshly ground black pepper			
Potatoes, diced and parboiled until just tender	450 g	I lb	I lb

① Heat the wok or a large heavy-based frying pan (skillet). Add the oil.

② When hot add the onion and garlic and stir-fry for 1 minute.

③ Add the pork and cook, stirring, for about 2 minutes or until all the meat has changed colour.

④ Stir in the mushrooms and apple cubes and cook for 2–3 minutes so that both have softened slightly.

⑤ Add the cider, chutney, mace, salt and pepper. Stir for 1 minute.

⑥ Gently mix in the cooked potato and heat through.

Serving suggestion: Serve hot on its own or with salad.

PREPARATION TIME: 10 MINUTES
COOKING TIME: 11 MINUTES

GAMMON AND CORN FRY

—— SERVES 4 ——

	METRIC	IMPERIAL	AMERICAN
Oil	15 ml	1 tbsp	1 tbsp
Onion, finely chopped	1	1	1
Gammon ham, cut into small cubes	350 g	12 oz	3 cups
Precooked potato, cut into small cubes	225 g	8 oz	8 oz
Canned or frozen sweetcorn (corn)	100 g	4 oz	4 oz
Cayenne pepper	2.5 ml	½ tsp	½ tsp
Salt and freshly ground black pepper			

① Heat the wok or a large heavy-based frying pan (skillet).

② Pour in the oil and when hot add the onion and stir-fry for 1 minute.

③ Add the ham and potato to the pan and cook for several minutes, being careful not to break up the potato.

④ Stir in the sweetcorn and cayenne pepper and season to taste. Cook for 1–2 minutes to ensure that the mixture is heated through.

Serving suggestion: Serve hot with crusty bread and a green salad.

PREPARATION TIME: 10 MINUTES
COOKING TIME: 6 MINUTES

GAMMON WITH PEACHES

—— SERVES 4 ——

	METRIC	IMPERIAL	AMERICAN
Oil	15 ml	1 tbsp	1 tbsp
Gammon steaks, cut into 2.5cm/1 in cubes	450 g	1 lb	1 lb
Can of peach slices, drained and syrup reserved	410 g	14½ oz	1 large
Mustard powder	5 ml	1 tsp	1 tsp
Paprika	2.5 ml	½ tsp	½ tsp
Cornflour (cornstarch)	5 ml	1 tsp	1 tsp
Salt and freshly ground black pepper			

① Heat the wok or a large heavy-based frying pan (skillet).

② Pour in the oil and when hot add the gammon and stir-fry for 3–4 minutes or until the meat is tender.

③ Stir in the peaches.

④ Combine the reserved peach syrup with water to make up to 90 ml/6 tbsp, then blend in the mustard powder, paprika and cornflour.

⑤ Pour the syrup mixture into the pan and cook, stirring, for 1–2 minutes until the sauce is slightly thickened. Season to taste.

Serving suggestion: Serve hot with crusty bread.

PREPARATION TIME: 5 MINUTES
COOKING TIME: 7 MINUTES

SAUSAGE WITH BABY POTATOES IN MUSTARD DRESSING
—— SERVES 4 ——

	METRIC	IMPERIAL	AMERICAN
Oil	30 ml	2 tbsp	2 tbsp
Garlic cloves, crushed	2	2	2
Large onion, sliced	1	1	1
Cooked sausage, cut into bite-size chunks	350 g	12 oz	12 oz
Precooked baby new potatoes	225 g	8 oz	8 oz
Wholegrain mustard	30 ml	2 tbsp	2 tbsp
Honey	15 ml	1 tbsp	1 tbsp
Extra virgin olive oil	15 ml	1 tbsp	1 tbsp
Salt and freshly ground black pepper			

① Heat the wok or a large heavy-based frying pan (skillet).

② Pour in the oil and when hot add the garlic and cook for 30 seconds.

③ Add the onion and stir-fry for 1 minute.

④ Add the sausage and potatoes and stir-fry for 3–4 minutes until the mixture is heated through.

⑤ Combine the mustard, honey, olive oil and seasoning and pour into the pan. Stir the mixture thoroughly and cook for a further minute.

Serving suggestion: Serve hot with a side salad.

PREPARATION TIME: 10 MINUTES
COOKING TIME: 8 MINUTES

POULTRY AND GAME DISHES

Chicken and poultry are quick and easy to cook and could have been designed especially for creating interesting dishes in the wok as they are so light and versatile. You can buy chicken already prepared in strips, cubes or goujons, but you will usually find it cheaper to buy larger portions and cut them up yourself. If you are using frozen chicken, make sure it is thoroughly thawed before cooking and always cook chicken and poultry thoroughly.

Experiment with different flavourings and mix and match with a range of colourful and healthy vegetables to extend your wok cookery even further.

SPICED CHICKEN WITH LENTILS AND CHILLIES
—— SERVES 4 ——

	METRIC	IMPERIAL	AMERICAN
Oil	30 ml	2 tbsp	2 tbsp
Garlic cloves, crushed	2	2	2
Chopped fresh root ginger	15 ml	1 tbsp	1 tbsp
Cardamom pods	3	3	3
Whole mild green chillies, slit	8	8	8
Chicken breasts, finely sliced	450 g	1 lb	1 lb
Precooked green lentils	100 g	4 oz	1 cup
Ground turmeric	2.5 ml	½ tsp	½ tsp
Ground cumin	2.5 ml	½ tsp	½ tsp
Salt	2.5 ml	½ tsp	½ tsp
Cherry tomatoes	12	12	12
Single (light) cream	150 ml	¼ pt	⅔ cup

① Heat the wok or a large heavy-based frying pan (skillet).

② Pour in the oil and when hot add the garlic, ginger and cardamom and stir-fry for a few seconds.

③ Add the chillies and chicken and cook for about 4 minutes.

④ Stir in the lentils and spices and cook for a few minutes.

⑤ Add the salt and tomatoes and stir-fry for 2 minutes.

⑥ Add the cream and heat through, stirring continuously.

Serving suggestion: Serve hot with boiled rice or naan bread.

PREPARATION TIME: 10 MINUTES
COOKING TIME: 12 MINUTES

MARYLAND-STYLE CHICKEN
—— SERVES 4 ——

	METRIC	IMPERIAL	AMERICAN
Cornflour (cornstarch)	10 ml	2 tsp	2 tsp
Cayenne pepper	2.5 ml	½ tsp	½ tsp
Water	5 ml	I tsp	I tsp
Worcestershire sauce	5 ml	I tsp	I tsp
Boneless chicken meat, cut into thin strips	450 g	I lb	I lb
Oil	30 ml	2 tbsp	2 tbsp
Baby sweetcorn (corn), fresh or thawed frozen	8	8	8
Bananas, sliced	2	2	2
Cashew nuts	15 ml	I tbsp	I tbsp

① Combine the cornflour with the cayenne pepper, water and Worcestershire sauce and pour over the chicken. Leave to marinate for 15 minutes.

② Heat the wok or a large heavy-based frying pan (skillet).

③ Pour in the oil and when hot add the chicken and sweetcorn and stir-fry for about 4 minutes or until the chicken is tender.

④ Gently stir in the bananas and nuts and heat through.

Serving suggestion: Serve hot with a crisp salad.

PREPARATION TIME: 5 MINUTES PLUS MARINATING
COOKING TIME: 7 MINUTES

BENGALI-STYLE CHICKEN

—— SERVES 4 ——

	METRIC	IMPERIAL	AMERICAN
Oil	30 ml	2 tbsp	2 tbsp
Garlic cloves, crushed	4	4	4
Chopped fresh root ginger	30 ml	2 tbsp	2 tbsp
Hot green chillies, finely diced	2	2	2
Large red onion, sliced	1	1	1
Boneless chicken meat, cut into strips	450 g	1 lb	1 lb
Large green (bell) pepper, sliced	1	1	1
Large ripe tomatoes, skinned and chopped	2	2	2
A pinch of sugar			
Salt	5 ml	1 tsp	1 tsp
Cayenne pepper	5 ml	1 tsp	1 tsp
Vinegar	15 ml	1 tbsp	1 tbsp

1. Heat the wok or a large heavy-based frying pan (skillet).
2. Pour in the oil and when hot add the garlic, ginger and chillies and cook for a few seconds.
3. Add the onion to the pan and cook for about 2 minutes or until it has softened slightly.
4. Stir in the chicken and cook for 3–4 minutes or until tender.
5. Add the green pepper and cook for about 30 seconds.
6. Add the remaining ingredients and stir for 3 minutes.

Serving suggestion: Serve hot with boiled rice or naan bread.

PREPARATION TIME: 15 MINUTES
COOKING TIME: 12 MINUTES

CHICKEN IN ASPARAGUS SAUCE
—— SERVES 4 ——

	METRIC	IMPERIAL	AMERICAN
Oil	15 ml	1 tbsp	1 tbsp
Small onion, finely chopped	1	1	1
Boneless chicken meat, cut into thin strips	450 g	1 lb	1 lb
Button mushrooms, quartered	50 g	2 oz	2 oz
Can of condensed asparagus soup	295 g	11 oz	1 med
Canned asparagus spears, cut into short lengths	8	8	8
Salt and freshly ground black pepper			

① Heat the wok or a large heavy-based frying pan (skillet).

② Pour in the oil and stir-fry the onion and chicken for 3–4 minutes or until the meat is tender.

③ Add the mushrooms and cook for 1 minute.

④ Gently stir in the undiluted soup and asparagus pieces.

⑤ Heat through, then season to taste and serve.

Serving suggestion: Serve hot with a selection of hot baby new vegetables.

PREPARATION TIME: 10 MINUTES
COOKING TIME: 10 MINUTES

CRUNCHY CHICKEN STIR-FRY
—— SERVES 4 ——

	METRIC	IMPERIAL	AMERICAN
Oil	15 ml	1 tbsp	1 tbsp
Garlic clove, crushed	1	1	1
Chopped fresh root ginger	5 ml	1 tsp	1 tsp
Spring onions (scallions), cut into short lengths	4	4	4
Boneless chicken meat, cut into thin strips	350 g	12 oz	12 oz
Mangetout (snow peas)	50 g	2 oz	2 oz
French (green) beans, cut into short lengths	50 g	2 oz	2 oz
Bamboo shoots, thinly sliced	50 g	2 oz	2 oz
Cashew nuts	50 g	2 oz	½ cup
A pinch of salt			
A pinch of sugar			
Soy sauce	15 ml	1 tbsp	1 tbsp
Sesame oil	10 ml	2 tsp	2 tsp

①   Heat the wok or a large heavy-based frying pan (skillet).

②   Pour in the oil and when hot add the garlic, ginger and spring onions and stir-fry for about 30 seconds.

③   Add the chicken and cook for about 3 minutes until tender.

④   Stir in the mangetout, beans and bamboo shoots and cook for 1 minute.

⑤   Add the remaining ingredients and stir for 1–2 minutes to ensure that the mixture is hot throughout.

Serving suggestion: Serve hot on its own or with noodles.

PREPARATION TIME: 15 MINUTES
COOKING TIME: 8 MINUTES

CHICKEN WITH ARTICHOKE HEARTS
—— SERVES 4 ——

	METRIC	IMPERIAL	AMERICAN
Oil	30 ml	2 tbsp	2 tbsp
Garlic clove, crushed	I	I	I
Small onion, finely chopped	I	I	I
Boneless chicken meat, thinly sliced	450 g	I lb	I lb
Mushrooms, quartered	100 g	4 oz	4 oz
Can of artichoke hearts, drained	400 g	14 oz	I large
Balsamic vinegar or red wine vinegar	15 ml	I tbsp	I tbsp
Brown sugar	10 ml	2 tsp	2 tsp
Lemon juice	5 ml	I tsp	I tsp
Salt and freshly ground black pepper			

① Heat the wok or a large heavy-based frying pan (skillet).

② Pour in the oil and when hot add the garlic and onion and stir-fry for about 30 seconds.

③ Add the chicken to the pan and cook for 3 minutes or until tender.

④ Add the mushrooms and cook for 1 minute.

⑤ Carefully stir in the remaining ingredients to avoid breaking up the artichoke hearts, then cook for several minutes to heat the mixture thoroughly.

Serving suggestion: Serve hot with a green salad.

PREPARATION TIME: 10 MINUTES
COOKING TIME: 8 MINUTES

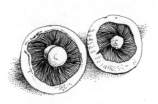

CHICKEN WITH OLIVES
—— SERVES 4 ——

	METRIC	IMPERIAL	AMERICAN
Oil	30 ml	2 tbsp	2 tbsp
Garlic cloves, crushed	4	4	4
Very small shallots or small pickling onions, halved	175 g	6 oz	6 oz
Chicken breasts, cut into fine strips	450 g	1 lb	1 lb
Mushrooms, quartered	100 g	4 oz	4 oz
White wine	150 ml	¼ pt	⅔ cup
Black olives, pitted (stoned)	100 g	4 oz	4 oz
Single (light) cream	30 ml	2 tbsp	2 tbsp
Salt and freshly ground black pepper			

① Heat the wok or a large heavy-based frying pan (skillet).

② Pour in the oil and when hot add the garlic and stir-fry for about 30 seconds.

③ Add the onions to the pan and stir-fry for about 3–4 minutes until they are quite soft.

④ Add the chicken and cook for 3 minutes or until tender.

⑤ Stir in the mushrooms and cook for 1 minute.

⑥ Pour in the wine and olives, bring the mixture to the boil and continue cooking for a minute or so to reduce the liquid.

⑦ Stir in the cream, season and heat through.

Serving suggestion: Serve hot with buttered noodles.

PREPARATION TIME: 15 MINUTES
COOKING TIME: 12 MINUTES

MIDDLE EASTERN-STYLE CHICKEN
—— SERVES 4 ——

	METRIC	IMPERIAL	AMERICAN
Garlic cloves	6	6	6
Oil	15 ml	1 tbsp	1 tbsp
Large onion, sliced	1	1	1
Boneless chicken meat, thinly sliced	450 g	1 lb	1 lb
Celery stick, sliced	1	1	1
Large green (bell) pepper, cut into thin strips	1	1	1
Large courgette (zucchini), cubed	1	1	1
Lemon, finely sliced and each slice quartered	1	1	1
Can of tomatoes	400 g	14 oz	1 large
Brown sugar	15 ml	1 tbsp	1 tbsp
Turmeric	10 ml	2 tsp	2 tsp
Chopped fresh oregano	30 ml	2 tbsp	2 tbsp
A sprig of thyme			
Salt and freshly ground black pepper			

① Cut 4 of the garlic cloves into slivers and crush the remaining 2.

② Heat the wok or a large heavy-based frying pan (skillet).

③ Pour in the oil and when hot add the garlic, onion and chicken and stir-fry for 2–4 minutes until the chicken is tender.

④ Add the celery, pepper, courgette and lemon and cook for 3 minutes.

⑤ Roughly chop the tomatoes, then add to the pan with the remaining ingredients, seasoning to taste.

⑥ Stir well, cover and simmer for about 10 minutes.

Serving suggestion: Serve hot with boiled rice.

PREPARATION TIME: 15 MINUTES
COOKING TIME: 20 MINUTES

SPICED CHICKEN MEATBALLS
—— SERVES 4 ——

	METRIC	IMPERIAL	AMERICAN
Cooked chicken meat, finely minced (ground)	350 g	12 oz	12 oz
Garlic cloves, crushed	2	2	2
Small onion, finely grated or minced (ground)	1	1	1
Very finely chopped fresh root ginger	15 ml	1 tbsp	1 tbsp
A pinch of fenugreek			
A pinch of ground cinnamon			
Ground cumin	2.5 ml	½ tsp	½ tsp
Chilli powder	2.5 ml	½ tsp	½ tsp
Ground cloves	2.5 ml	½ tsp	½ tsp
Salt	1.5 ml	¼ tsp	¼ tsp
Natural yoghurt	10 ml	2 tsp	2 tsp
Oil	60 ml	4 tbsp	4 tbsp

1. Combine the chicken, garlic, onion, spices and salt.

2. Stir in half the yoghurt and if the mixture seems too dry add a little more to bind it. Form the mixture into walnut-sized balls.

3. Heat the wok or a large heavy-based frying pan (skillet).

4. Pour in the oil and when very hot fry (sauté) the meatballs a few at a time, stirring very gently all the time. Cook for 2–3 minutes or until they are browned all over.

5. Lift the balls out with a draining spoon, place on kitchen paper (paper towels) and keep warm while you cook the remaining meatballs.

Serving suggestion: Serve hot or cold with green salad or pickle.

PREPARATION TIME: 10 MINUTES
COOKING TIME: 12 MINUTES

SPICY CHICKEN LIVERS

—— SERVES 4 ——

	METRIC	IMPERIAL	AMERICAN
Plain (all-purpose) flour	15 ml	1 tbsp	1 tbsp
Chilli powder	5 ml	1 tsp	1 tsp
Ground cumin	2.5 ml	½ tsp	½ tsp
Curry powder	2.5 ml	½ tsp	½ tsp
Salt and freshly ground black pepper			
Chicken livers, sliced	450 g	1 lb	1 lb
Oil	30 ml	2 tbsp	2 tbsp
Garlic cloves, crushed	2	2	2
Shallot, finely chopped	1	1	1
Small red chilli, very finely chopped	1	1	1
Chopped fresh coriander (cilantro)	15 ml	1 tbsp	1 tbsp

① Combine the flour, spices, salt and pepper and use to coat the chicken livers.

② Heat the wok or a large heavy-based frying pan (skillet).

③ Pour in the oil and when very hot add the garlic, shallot and chilli and stir-fry for about 30 seconds.

④ Add the chicken livers to the pan and carefully stir-fry for 2–3 minutes until they are crisp on the outside and the juices are no longer bloody.

⑤ Sprinkle with the fresh coriander.

Serving suggestion: Serve hot with cucumber salad.

PREPARATION TIME: 10 MINUTES
COOKING TIME: 5 MINUTES

CRANBERRY TURKEY

—— SERVES 4 ——

	METRIC	IMPERIAL	AMERICAN
Turkey breast, sliced	450 g	1 lb	1 lb
Plain (all-purpose) flour	30 ml	2 tbsp	2 tbsp
Oil	30 ml	2 tbsp	2 tbsp
Onion, finely chopped	1	1	1
Fresh thyme sprigs	4	4	4
Cranberry jelly (clear conserve)	60 ml	4 tbsp	4 tbsp
Port or sweet sherry	45 ml	3 tbsp	3 tbsp
Salt and freshly ground black pepper			

① Dip the turkey in the flour.

② Heat the wok or a large heavy-based frying pan (skillet).

③ Pour in the oil and when hot add the floured turkey, onion and thyme and stir-fry for about 3 minutes or until the turkey is tender.

④ Stir in the cranberry jelly and port or sherry. Season to taste.

⑤ Cook for several minutes until the sauce has thickened. If the sauce seems too thick, add a little water.

Serving suggestion: Serve hot with a selection of fresh vegetables.

PREPARATION TIME: 10 MINUTES
COOKING TIME: 8 MINUTES

TURKEY WITH NOODLES

—— SERVES 4 ——

	METRIC	IMPERIAL	AMERICAN
Turkey breast, thinly sliced	350 g	12 oz	12 oz
Plain (all-purpose) flour, seasoned	30 ml	2 tbsp	2 tbsp
Oil	15 ml	1 tbsp	1 tbsp
Small shallots, finely chopped	2	2	2
Button mushrooms, sliced	100 g	4 oz	4 oz
Chopped fresh thyme	10 ml	2 tsp	2 tsp
Dry vermouth	45 ml	3 tbsp	3 tbsp
Single (light) cream	150 ml	¼ pt	⅔ cup
Salt and freshly ground black pepper			
Cooked green tagliatelle	100 g	4 oz	4 oz

① Coat the turkey in the seasoned flour.

② Heat the wok or a large heavy-based frying pan (skillet).

③ Pour in the oil and when hot add the turkey and shallots. Stir-fry for 3–4 minutes until the meat is tender.

④ Add the mushrooms and thyme and cook for 1 minute.

⑤ Sprinkle any remaining flour over the surface of the contents of the pan and stir in well.

⑥ Gradually blend in the vermouth and cream and cook, stirring, until the sauce is slightly thickened.

⑦ Season to taste, then stir in the tagliatelle and ensure that the mixture is heated through.

Serving suggestion: Serve hot with a crisp salad.

PREPARATION TIME: 10 MINUTES
COOKING TIME: 10 MINUTES

TURKEY WITH LEEKS

—— SERVES 4 ——

	METRIC	IMPERIAL	AMERICAN
Oil	30 ml	2 tbsp	2 tbsp
Leeks, finely sliced	2	2	2
Shallot, finely chopped	1	1	1
Turkey breast, finely sliced	450 g	1 lb	1 lb
Plain (all-purpose) flour, seasoned	30 ml	2 tbsp	2 tbsp
Chicken stock	60 ml	4 tbsp	4 tbsp
Single (light) cream	150 ml	¼ pt	⅔ cup
Cheddar cheese, grated	50 g	2 oz	½ cup
A pinch of grated nutmeg			
Salt and freshly ground black pepper			

① Heat the wok or a large heavy-based frying pan (skillet).

② Pour in the oil and heat, then add the leeks and shallot and stir-fry for about 2 minutes or until they are softened.

③ Dip the turkey strips in the seasoned flour, then add to the pan and cook for 3–4 minutes to tenderise the meat.

④ Pour in the stock and cream and cook, stirring constantly, until the sauce is slightly thickened.

⑤ Add the cheese and stir the mixture until it melts.

⑥ Add the nutmeg and season to taste.

Serving suggestion: Serve hot with mashed potato.

PREPARATION TIME: 10 MINUTES
COOKING TIME: 10 MINUTES

TURKEY IN DAMSON SAUCE
—— SERVES 4 ——

	METRIC	IMPERIAL	AMERICAN
Oil	15 ml	1 tbsp	1 tbsp
Garlic clove, crushed	1	1	1
Large red onion, chopped	1	1	1
Boneless turkey meat, cut into fine strips	450 g	1 lb	1 lb
Damson jam (jelly)	45 ml	3 tbsp	3 tbsp
Chicken stock	150 ml	¼ pt	⅔ cup
Salt and freshly ground black pepper			

① Heat the wok or a large heavy-based frying pan (skillet).

② Pour in the oil and when hot add the garlic and onion and cook for about 1 minute.

③ Add the turkey to the pan and stir-fry for several minutes until tender.

④ Stir in the jam and stock and boil to reduce the volume of liquid slightly and produce a syrupy sauce. Season to taste.

Serving suggestion: Serve hot with fresh vegetables.

PREPARATION TIME: 10 MINUTES
COOKING TIME: 8 MINUTES

DUCK WITH CHERRIES

—— SERVES 4 ——

	METRIC	IMPERIAL	AMERICAN
Oil	30 ml	2 tbsp	2 tbsp
Shallots, finely chopped	2	2	2
Boneless duck meat, cut into fine strips	350 g	12 oz	12 oz
Can of stoned (pitted) black cherries, drained and syrup reserved	410 g	14½ oz	1 large
Cornflour (cornstarch)	10 ml	2 tsp	2 tsp
Water	60 ml	4 tbsp	4 tbsp
Sweet sherry	15 ml	1 tbsp	1 tbsp

① Heat the wok or a large heavy-based frying pan (skillet).

② Pour in the oil and when hot stir-fry the shallots for about 1 minute.

③ Add the duck to the pan and stir-fry for 3–4 minutes or until tender.

④ Add the cherries and stir well.

⑤ Blend the cornflour with the water, then mix in the sherry and about 60 ml/4 tbsp of the reserved cherry syrup.

⑥ Pour into the pan and cook, stirring, for several minutes until the sauce thickens.

Serving suggestion: Serve hot with a selection of seasonable vegetables.

PREPARATION TIME: 10 MINUTES
COOKING TIME: 10 MINUTES

PEKING-STYLE DUCK

—— SERVES 4 ——

	METRIC	IMPERIAL	AMERICAN
Soy sauce	10 ml	2 tsp	2 tsp
Dry sherry	10 ml	2 tsp	2 tsp
A pinch of Chinese five-spice powder			
Boneless duck meat, cut into thin strips	450 g	1 lb	1 lb
Oil	30 ml	2 tbsp	2 tbsp
Garlic clove, crushed	1	1	1
Spring onions (scallions), finely shredded	4	4	4
Cucumber, peeled, seeded and cut into short sticks	50 g	2 oz	2 oz
Hoisin sauce	30 ml	2 tbsp	2 tbsp

① Combine the soy sauce, sherry and five-spice powder and use to marinate the duck for 15 minutes.

② Heat the wok or a large heavy-based frying pan (skillet).

③ Pour in the oil and when hot add the garlic and stir-fry for 30 seconds.

④ Add the duck, reserving the marinade, and cook for about 3 minutes or until tender.

⑤ Add the spring onions and cucumber and cook for 1 minute.

⑥ Stir in the hoisin sauce and the remaining marinade and heat the duck mixture through thoroughly.

Serving suggestion: Serve hot with rice or Chinese pancakes.

PREPARATION TIME: 10 MINUTES PLUS MARINATING
COOKING TIME: 7 MINUTES

RABBIT WITH PRUNES
—— SERVES 4 ——

	METRIC	IMPERIAL	AMERICAN
Boneless rabbit, cut into strips	350 g	12 oz	12 oz
Plain (all-purpose) flour, seasoned	30 ml	2 tbsp	2 tbsp
Oil	30 ml	2 tbsp	2 tbsp
Garlic cloves, thinly sliced	3	3	3
Shallots, quartered	8	8	8
Celery stick, sliced	1	1	1
Dried stoned (pitted) prunes, soaked and halved	8	8	8
Green peppercorns, crushed	5 ml	1 tsp	1 tsp
Chicken stock	300 ml	½ pt	1¼ cups
Salt			

① Coat the rabbit with the seasoned flour.

② Heat the wok or a large heavy-based frying pan (skillet).

③ Pour in the oil and heat, then add the garlic, shallots and celery and cook for about 1–2 minutes until slightly softened.

④ Add the rabbit to the pan and stir-fry for about 3 minutes until tender.

⑤ Stir in the prunes and peppercorns with any remaining flour.

⑥ Gradually blend in the stock, bring to the boil and cook, stirring, until the gravy is slightly thickened. Add salt to taste.

Serving suggestion: Serve hot with seasonable vegetables.

PREPARATION TIME: 5 MINUTES PLUS SOAKING
COOKING TIME: 10 MINUTES

JUNIPER VENISON
—— SERVES 4 ——

	METRIC	IMPERIAL	AMERICAN
Oil	15 ml	1 tbsp	1 tbsp
Garlic cloves, finely sliced	3	3	3
Shallots, quartered	8	8	8
Celery sticks, finely sliced	2	2	2
Boneless venison meat, cut into thin strips	350 g	12 oz	12 oz
Plain (all-purpose) flour, seasoned	30 ml	2 tbsp	2 tbsp
Juniper berries, crushed	10 ml	2 tsp	2 tsp
Green peppercorns, crushed	5 ml	1 tsp	1 tsp
Finely grated orange rind	5 ml	1 tsp	1 tsp
Orange juice	30 ml	2 tbsp	2 tbsp
Beef stock	300 ml	½ pt	1¼ cups
Salt			

① Heat the wok or a large heavy-based frying pan (skillet).

② Pour in the oil and when hot stir-fry the garlic and shallots for about 1 minute.

③ Add the celery to the pan and cook for 1 minute.

④ Dip the venison quickly in the seasoned flour and add to the pan, stir-frying for 3–4 minutes or until the meat is tender.

⑤ Stir in the juniper berries, peppercorns and orange zest and cook for a few seconds.

⑥ Sprinkle any remaining flour over the meat mixture and stir it in.

⑦ Stirring constantly, gradually blend in the orange juice and beef stock. Cook for a few minutes to thicken the gravy slightly and add salt to taste.

Serving suggestion: Serve hot with roast potatoes and vegetables.

PREPARATION TIME: 15 MINUTES
COOKING TIME: 10 MINUTES

VEGETABLE DISHES

The next best thing to the texture and nutritional value of raw vegetables is to have them lightly stir-fried. But if you prefer your vegetables traditionally tender, they can be stir-fried first and then braised in the wok in any number of sauces and gravies. Although the 'Chinese' varieties of vegetables are great stir-fried, don't forget the good old British veg, which can take on a whole new character when given the wok treatment! Similarly, there are vegetables from all round the world that can be cooked in the wok to acquire a completely new image.

Frozen and canned vegetables can be used in stir-fries, but fresh seasonal vegetables really come into their own when cooked by this method and are a must for those with an eye to healthy eating.

Most of the dishes in this chapter are meals in their own right; some make excellent accompaniments to other more substantial dishes. And feel free to experiment and add some strips of meat or fish to some of the recipes.

COCONUT CHICK PEAS

—— SERVES 4 ——

	METRIC	IMPERIAL	AMERICAN
Oil	15 ml	1 tbsp	1 tbsp
Garlic cloves, crushed	2	2	2
Onion, finely chopped	1	1	1
Mild green chillies, cut into fine strips	2	2	2
Cumin seeds	2.5 ml	½ tsp	½ tsp
Fenugreek seeds	2.5 ml	½ tsp	½ tsp
Salt	2.5 ml	½ tsp	½ tsp
Can of chick peas (garbanzos), drained	440 g	15½ oz	1 large
Canned coconut milk	150 ml	¼ pt	⅔ cup
Chopped fresh coriander (cilantro)	15 ml	1 tbsp	1 tbsp

①   Heat the wok or a large heavy-based frying pan (skillet)

②   Pour in the oil and when hot add the garlic, onion, chillies and spice seeds and stir-fry for about 1 minute.

③   Add the salt, chick peas and coconut milk. Reduce the heat slightly, cover and cook for 3–5 minutes.

④   Serve hot, sprinkled with the coriander.

PREPARATION TIME: 10 MINUTES
COOKING TIME: 8 MINUTES

PARSNIPS WITH CASHEWS AND PARMESAN
—— SERVES 4 ——

	METRIC	IMPERIAL	AMERICAN
Oil	30 ml	2 tbsp	2 tbsp
Parboiled parsnips, cut into fine, short lengths	450 g	1 lb	1 lb
Cashew nuts	50 g	2 oz	½ cup
Very finely grated Parmesan cheese	30 ml	2 tbsp	2 tbsp
Celery salt	2.5 ml	½ tsp	½ tsp
Ground black pepper			

① Heat the wok or a large heavy-based frying pan (skillet).

② Pour in the oil and when hot add the parsnips and stir-fry for 2–3 minutes or until they are tender and lightly tinged brown.

③ Stir in the nuts and cook for 1 minute.

④ Add the cheese, celery salt and pepper to taste. Stir well and serve hot.

PREPARATION TIME: 5 MINUTES
COOKING TIME: 6 MINUTES

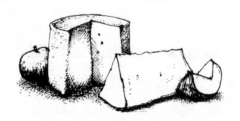

FRENCH BEANS WITH BACON

—— SERVES 4 ——

	METRIC	IMPERIAL	AMERICAN
Oil	15 ml	1 tbsp	1 tbsp
Small onion, finely chopped	1	1	1
Smoked bacon, finely chopped	50 g	2 oz	2 oz
French (green) beans, trimmed and cut into short lengths	450 g	1 lb	1 lb
Salt and freshly ground black pepper			

1. Heat the wok or a large heavy-based frying pan (skillet).
2. Pour in the oil and when hot add the onion and stir-fry for about 30 seconds.
3. Add the bacon and stir-fry for 2–3 minutes until slightly crisp.
4. Stir in the beans and cook for 3–5 minutes until tender.
5. Season to taste and serve hot.

PREPARATION TIME: 10 MINUTES
COOKING TIME: 9 MINUTES

SUMMER SALAD STIR-FRY
—— SERVES 4 ——

	METRIC	IMPERIAL	AMERICAN
Groundnut (peanut) oil	15 ml	1 tbsp	1 tbsp
Garlic clove, crushed	1	1	1
French (green) beans, cut into short lengths	100 g	4 oz	4 oz
Spring onions (scallions), finely chopped	5	5	5
Large celery stick, chopped	1	1	1
Courgette (zucchini), cut into short sticks	1	1	1
Chinese leaves, finely shredded	2	2	2
Honey	15 ml	1 tbsp	1 tbsp
Lemon juice	15 ml	1 tbsp	1 tbsp
Salt and freshly ground black pepper			
Sesame seeds	15 ml	1 tbsp	1 tbsp

1. Heat the wok or a large heavy-based frying pan (skillet).
2. Add the oil. When hot add the garlic, beans, onions, celery and courgette and stir-fry for about 2 minutes until the beans are slightly softened.
3. Stir in the Chinese leaves.
4. Add the honey, lemon juice, seasoning and sesame seeds.
5. Stir well and serve hot.

PREPARATION TIME: 10 MINUTES
COOKING TIME: 5 MINUTES

CELERY IN BRIE AND CHIVE SAUCE

—— SERVES 4 ——

	METRIC	IMPERIAL	AMERICAN
Oil	15 ml	1 tbsp	1 tbsp
Shallots, finely chopped	2	2	2
Celery, finely sliced	450 g	1 lb	1 lb
Single (light) cream	150 ml	¼ pt	⅔ cup
Blue Brie, cubed	150 g	5 oz	1¼ cups
Salt and freshly ground black pepper			
Chopped fresh chives	15 ml	1 tbsp	1 tbsp

① Heat the wok or a large heavy-based frying pan (skillet).

② Pour in the oil and when hot add the shallots and celery and stir-fry for about 3 minutes or until the celery is quite tender.

③ Add the cream, then sprinkle in the cheese and stir until it is all melted.

④ Season to taste and serve hot with the chives scattered over the top.

PREPARATION TIME: 10 MINUTES
COOKING TIME: 5 MINUTES

STIR-FRIED BROCCOLI AND CAULIFLOWER

—— SERVES 4 ——

	METRIC	IMPERIAL	AMERICAN
Oil	30 ml	2 tbsp	2 tbsp
Garlic cloves, crushed	2	2	2
Chopped fresh root ginger	15 ml	1 tbsp	1 tbsp
Fresh mild green chilli, finely chopped	1	1	1
Cauliflower florets, thinly sliced	225 g	8 oz	8 oz
Broccoli florets, thinly sliced	225 g	8 oz	8 oz
Soy sauce	15 ml	1 tbsp	1 tbsp
Dry sherry	15 ml	1 tbsp	1 tbsp
A pinch of sugar			
Salted peanuts, roughly crushed	25 g	1 oz	¼ cup

① Heat the wok or a large heavy-based frying pan (skillet).

② Pour in the oil and when hot add the garlic, ginger and chilli and cook for about 30 seconds.

③ Add the cauliflower and broccoli and stir-fry for 3–4 minutes until both are slightly softened.

④ Stir in the soy sauce, sherry and sugar and heat the mixture through.

⑤ Serve hot with the peanuts scattered over the top.

PREPARATION TIME: 10 MINUTES
COOKING TIME: 6 MINUTES

SPINACH WITH ALMONDS

—— SERVES 4 ——

	METRIC	IMPERIAL	AMERICAN
Oil	15 ml	1 tbsp	1 tbsp
Small onion, finely chopped	1	1	1
Garlic cloves, finely sliced	4	4	4
Spinach, hard stalks removed and roughly chopped	750 g	1½ lb	1½ lb
Soy sauce	15 ml	1 tbsp	1 tbsp
A pinch of sugar			
Flaked (slivered) almonds	50 g	2 oz	½ cup
A pinch of freshly ground black pepper			

① Heat the wok or a large heavy-based frying pan (skillet).

② Pour in the oil and when hot stir-fry the onion and garlic for 30–60 seconds until lightly browned.

③ Add the spinach and stir for about 2 minutes until wilted.

④ Stir in the remaining ingredients and cook for a further 2 minutes. Serve hot.

PREPARATION TIME: 10 MINUTES

COOKING TIME: 5 MINUTES

CURRIED VEGETABLES
—— SERVES 4 ——

	METRIC	IMPERIAL	AMERICAN
Large carrots, thickly sliced	3	3	3
Large courgettes (zucchini), thickly sliced	2	2	2
Celery sticks, cut into short lengths	2	2	2
Oil	30 ml	2 tbsp	2 tbsp
Garlic cloves, crushed	2	2	2
Chopped fresh root ginger	15 ml	1 tbsp	1 tbsp
Large onion, sliced	1	1	1
Small red (bell) pepper, sliced	1	1	1
Button mushrooms	50 g	2 oz	2 oz
Medium-hot curry paste, from a jar or can	45 ml	3 tbsp	3 tbsp
Canned coconut milk	150 ml	¼ pt	⅔ cup
Water	150 ml	¼ pt	⅔ cup
Chopped fresh coriander (cilantro)	15 ml	1 tbsp	1 tbsp

① Bring a saucepan of water to the boil, then immerse the carrots and cook for 2 of minutes.

② Add the courgettes and celery and cook for 1 minute. Drain well.

③ Heat the wok or a large heavy-based frying pan (skillet).

④ Pour in the oil and when hot stir-fry the garlic and ginger for a few seconds.

⑤ Add the onion and red pepper and stir-fry for 1 minute.

⑥ Add the parboiled vegetables to the pan with the mushrooms and cook, stirring, for about 3 minutes or until all the vegetables are quite tender.

⑦ Stir in the curry paste followed by the coconut milk and water and cook for a further 3 minutes so that all the ingredients are hot and the sauce slightly thickened.

⑧ Serve garnished with the coriander.

PREPARATION TIME: 15 MINUTES
COOKING TIME: 15 MINUTES

LEMON CARROTS
—— SERVES 4 ——

	METRIC	IMPERIAL	AMERICAN
Oil	15 ml	1 tbsp	1 tbsp
Shallot, very finely chopped	1	1	1
Carrots, cut into thin, short sticks	450 g	1 lb	1 lb
Lemon juice	45 ml	3 tbsp	3 tbsp
Finely grated lemon zest	15 ml	1 tbsp	1 tbsp
Soft brown sugar	15 ml	1 tbsp	1 tbsp

① Heat the wok or a large heavy-based frying pan (skillet).

② Pour in the oil and when hot add the shallot and cook for 30 seconds.

③ Add the carrots and stir-fry for 3–4 minutes until slightly softened.

④ Stir in the lemon juice, zest and sugar.

⑤ Heat through and serve hot.

PREPARATION TIME: 5 MINUTES
COOKING TIME: 6 MINUTES

TOFU WITH MEDITERRANEAN VEGETABLES

—— SERVES 4 ——

	METRIC	IMPERIAL	AMERICAN
Aubergine (eggplant), cubed	I	I	I
Salt and white pepper			
Tofu, drained and cut into 1 cm/½ in cubes	2 × 285 g packs	2 × 10½ oz packs	2 × 10½ oz packs
Oil	30 ml	2 tbsp	2 tbsp
Garlic cloves, crushed	2	2	2
Large onion, sliced	I	I	I
Small red (bell) pepper, thinly sliced	I	I	I
Small green pepper, thinly sliced	I	I	I
Courgette (zucchini), sliced	I	I	I
Large tomatoes, skinned and chopped	3	3	3
Torn basil leaves	30 ml	2 tbsp	2 tbsp
Tomato purée (paste)	30 ml	2 tbsp	2 tbsp
Mozzarella cheese, cut into small cubes	50 g	2 oz	½ cup

① Place the aubergine cubes on a plate and sprinkle with salt. Leave for 20 minutes, then rinse under cold running water.

② Coat the tofu cubes with salt and pepper.

③ Heat the wok or a large heavy-based frying pan (skillet).

④ Pour in the oil and when hot add the tofu and stir-fry for approximately 4 minutes or until it is browned all over.

⑤ Add the garlic, onion, peppers and aubergine to the pan and continue to stir-fry for about 4 minutes until the vegetables are softened.

⑥ Stir in the courgette and tomatoes and cook for 1–2 minutes.

⑦ Add the basil leaves and tomato purée. Season to taste and heat through.

⑧   Spoon into individual heatproof bowls and sprinkle the cubed Mozzarella over the top.

⑨   Place under a very hot grill (broiler) for a few seconds to melt and slightly brown the cheese. Serve hot.

PREPARATION TIME: 15 MINUTES PLUS SALTING
COOKING TIME: 15 MINUTES

SUGARED GREEN TOMATOES
—— SERVES 4 ——

	METRIC	IMPERIAL	AMERICAN
Oil	15 ml	I tbsp	I tbsp
Green tomatoes, thinly sliced	450 g	I lb	I lb
Demerara sugar	30 ml	2 tbsp	2 tbsp

①   Heat the wok or a large heavy-based frying pan (skillet).

②   Add the oil and when hot add the tomatoes and stir-fry for about 3 minutes or until they are softened but still retain some shape.

③   Carefully stir in the sugar and serve hot.

PREPARATION TIME: 3 MINUTES
COOKING TIME: 4 MINUTES

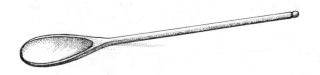

CHICORY WITH PEARS
—— SERVES 4 ——

	METRIC	IMPERIAL	AMERICAN
Oil	15 ml	I tbsp	I tbsp
Small red onion, finely chopped	I	I	I
Chicory (Belgian endive) heads, finely sliced crosswise	3	3	3
Firm pears, peeled, cored and diced	3	3	3
Balsamic vinegar	30 ml	2 tbsp	2 tbsp
A pinch of sugar			
A pinch of ground cloves			
Salt and freshly ground black pepper			

① Heat the wok or a large heavy-based frying pan (skillet).

② Heat the oil, then add the onion and stir-fryfor about 1 minute.

③ Add the chicory and pears and stir-fry for 2 minutes or until the chicory is just slightly softened.

④ Stir in the vinegar, sugar and cloves, then season to taste. Heat through and serve hot.

PREPARATION TIME: 10 MINUTES

COOKING TIME: 5 MINUTES

FRESH VEGETABLE STIR-FRY
—— SERVES 4 ——

	METRIC	IMPERIAL	AMERICAN
Oil	15 ml	1 tbsp	1 tbsp
Garlic cloves, crushed	2	2	2
Chopped fresh root ginger	15 ml	1 tbsp	1 tbsp
Spring onions (scallions), chopped	4	4	4
Mangetout (snow peas), trimmed	225 g	8 oz	8 oz
Baby sweetcorn (corn), fresh or thawed frozen	12	12	12
Button mushrooms, quartered	100 g	4 oz	4 oz
Soy sauce	15 ml	1 tbsp	1 tbsp
Oyster sauce	15 ml	1 tbsp	1 tbsp
A pinch of sugar			

① Heat the wok or a large heavy-based frying pan (skillet).

② Pour in the oil and when hot add the garlic and ginger and cook for a few seconds.

③ Add the spring onions, mangetout, sweetcorn and mushrooms and stir-fry for about 2 minutes so that they are all slightly softened.

④ Stir in the remaining ingredients and cook for 1 minute, then serve hot.

PREPARATION TIME: 10 MINUTES
COOKING TIME: 4 MINUTES

BRUSSELS AND CHESTNUTS WITH PORT
—— SERVES 4 ——

	METRIC	IMPERIAL	AMERICAN
Oil	15 ml	1 tbsp	1 tbsp
Small shallot, chopped	1	1	1
Brussels sprouts, parboiled and halved	450 g	1 lb	1 lb
Whole canned chestnuts, shelled and drained	100 g	4 oz	4 oz
A pinch of ground cinnamon			
Port	15 ml	1 tbsp	1 tbsp
Salt and freshly ground black pepper			

① Heat the wok or a large heavy-based frying pan (skillet).

② Pour in the oil and when hot add the shallot and stir-fry for about 1 minute until it is soft.

③ Add the Brussels sprouts to the pan and cook for 2–3 minutes.

④ Stir in the chestnuts, cinnamon and port and season to taste.

⑤ Cook for another 1–2 minutes to heat through, then serve.

PREPARATION TIME: 5 MINUTES
COOKING TIME: 7 MINUTES

LEEKS WITH FRESH HERBS

—— SERVES 4 ——

	METRIC	IMPERIAL	AMERICAN
Oil	15 ml	1 tbsp	1 tbsp
Leeks, finely sliced	3	3	3
Green (bell) pepper, diced	1	1	1
Chopped fresh thyme	10 ml	2 tsp	2 tsp
Chopped fresh parsley	15 ml	1 tbsp	1 tbsp
Chopped fresh sage	5 ml	1 tsp	1 tsp
Chopped fresh rosemary	5 ml	1 tsp	1 tsp
Vegetable stock	60 ml	4 tbsp	4 tbsp
Salt and freshly ground black pepper			

① Heat the wok or a large heavy-based frying pan (skillet).

② Pour in the oil and when hot add the leeks and green pepper and stir-fry for about 4 minutes.

③ Stir in the herbs and cook for 1 minute.

④ Add the stock and season to taste. Heat through and serve.

PREPARATION TIME: 15 MINUTES
COOKING TIME: 9 MINUTES

CHUTNEY-STYLE VEGETABLES

—— SERVES 4 ——

	METRIC	IMPERIAL	AMERICAN
Oil	30 ml	2 tbsp	2 tbsp
Garlic clove, crushed	I	I	I
Chopped fresh root ginger	10 ml	2 tsp	2 tsp
Small red chilli, finely chopped	I	I	I
Onion, chopped	I	I	I
Marrow (squash), peeled, seeded and finely cubed	225 g	8 oz	8 oz
Eating (dessert) apples, peeled, cored and finely cubed	2	2	2
Red (bell) pepper, diced	I	I	I
Brown sugar	30 ml	2 tbsp	2 tbsp
White wine vinegar	30 ml	2 tbsp	2 tbsp
A pinch of ground allspice			
Salt and freshly ground black pepper			

① Heat the wok or a large heavy-based frying pan (skillet).

② Pour in the oil and when hot add the garlic, ginger and chilli and cook for 30 seconds.

③ Place the onion in the pan and stir-fry for 1 minute.

④ Add the marrow, apple and red pepper and cook, stirring, for 4–5 minutes or until all the vegetables are quite soft.

⑤ Stir in the remaining ingredients, season to taste and cook for a further 2–3 minutes before serving.

Serving suggestion: Serve hot with cold meats.

PREPARATION TIME: 15 MINUTES
COOKING TIME: 12 MINUTES

STIR-FRIED CUCUMBER
—— SERVES 4 ——

	METRIC	IMPERIAL	AMERICAN
Cucumbers, peeled, seeded and cut into short sticks	1½	1½	1½
Salt			
Oil	15 ml	1 tbsp	1 tbsp
Garlic clove, crushed	1	1	1
Chopped fresh ginger	5 ml	1 tsp	1 tsp
Black bean sauce	15 ml	1 tbsp	1 tbsp
A pinch of Chinese five-spice powder			
Soy sauce	10 ml	2 tsp	2 tsp
Dry sherry	5 ml	1 tsp	1 tsp
A pinch of sugar			

① Place the cucumber on a plate and sprinkle with salt. Leave for 20 minutes to remove any excess liquid, then rinse in cold water and pat dry with kitchen paper (paper towels).

② Heat the wok or a large heavy-based frying pan (skillet).

③ Pour in the oil and when hot add the garlic and ginger and cook for a few seconds.

④ Add the cucumber to the pan and stir-fry for a further few seconds.

⑤ Stir in all the remaining ingredients and cook for 3 minutes. Serve hot.

PREPARATION TIME: 10 MINUTES PLUS SALTING
COOKING TIME: 5 MINUTES

TOFU WITH MUSHROOMS

—— SERVES 4 ——

	METRIC	IMPERIAL	AMERICAN
Small red chilli, finely chopped	I	I	I
Soy sauce	15 ml	I tbsp	I tbsp
Vinegar	15 ml	I tbsp	I tbsp
A pinch of Chinese five-spice powder			
Garlic cloves, crushed	3	3	3
Tofu, drained and thinly sliced	285 g pack	10½ oz pack	10½ oz pack
Oil	15 ml	I tbsp	I tbsp
Large onion, finely sliced	I	I	I
Button mushrooms, quartered	225 g	8 oz	8 oz

① Combine the chilli, soy sauce, vinegar, spice and garlic and use to marinate the tofu for about 10 minutes.

② Heat the wok or a large heavy-based frying pan (skillet).

③ Pour in the oil and when hot stir-fry the onion for 1 minute.

④ Reserving the marinade, add the tofu to the pan and stir-fry for about 5 minutes or until quite brown all over.

⑤ Add the mushrooms to the pan and cook for 1 minute.

⑥ Stir in the reserved marinade and cook for 2–3 minutes. Serve hot.

PREPARATION TIME: 5 MINUTES PLUS MARINATING

COOKING TIME: 10 MINUTES

SNACKS

The wok is only now becoming appreciated as a utensil in which to cook snack meals, mainly as a result of cookery programmes that show quick snacks being prepared in woks on the streets of India and other Asian countries.

Try stir-frying nuts, pulses and wafer-thin slices of root vegetables – potato, carrot, beetroot (red beet) or parsnip – then seasoning with salt for quick, nutritious nibbles. Make the most of your storecupboard foods, such as cans and packet goods, and leftover vegetables to create unexpectedly tasty snacks. Stir-fry some strips of bacon or slices of sausage, then stir in beaten eggs to make an exciting variation on scrambled eggs. Or stir-fry leftover slices of cooked potatoes and add a few prawns (shrimp) and some curry paste or spices to make a quick and exciting meal.

CREAMED CORN TOASTS

—— SERVES 4 ——

	METRIC	IMPERIAL	AMERICAN
Oil	30 ml	2 tbsp	2 tbsp
Small onion, finely chopped	I	I	I
Herby sausages, cut into bite-sized pieces	450 g	I lb	I lb
Can of creamed sweetcorn (corn)	300 g	I I oz	I large
Salt and freshly ground black pepper			
Thick slices of wholemeal bread, toasted	4	4	4

① Heat the wok or a large heavy-based frying pan (skillet).

② Pour in the oil and when hot stir-fry the onion for 1 minute.

③ Add the sausages and stir-fry for about 4 minutes or until browned and cooked on the inside.

④ Drain any excess oil from the pan, then add the creamed sweetcorn. Season to taste, then stir and heat the mixture through.

⑤ Divide the mixture between the slices of toast and serve.

PREPARATION TIME: 5 MINUTES
COOKING TIME: 7 MINUTES

SWEET SPICED NUTS

—— SERVES 4 ——

	METRIC	IMPERIAL	AMERICAN
Oil	60 ml	4 tbsp	4 tbsp
Blanched almonds	100 g	4 oz	1 cup
Large shelled peanuts	100 g	4 oz	1 cup
Cashew nuts	100 g	4 oz	1 cup
Walnut halves	100 g	4 oz	1 cup
Soft brown sugar	30 ml	2 tbsp	2 tbsp
Grated nutmeg	2.5 ml	½ tsp	½ tsp
Ground cinnamon	10 ml	2 tsp	2 tsp

①   Heat the wok or a large heavy-based frying pan (skillet).

②   Add the oil and when very hot add all the nuts and stir-fry for about 2–3 minutes until they are browned.

③   Drain off any excess oil, then return to the heat and stir in the sugar and spices.

④   Serve warm or cold as a dish of nibbles to go with drinks. Can be stored in a screw-top jar.

PREPARATION TIME: NONE

COOKING TIME: 4 MINUTES

FIVE-MINUTE FRIED RICE

—— SERVES 4 ——

	METRIC	IMPERIAL	AMERICAN
Oil	30 ml	2 tbsp	2 tbsp
Cold precooked long-grain rice	450 g	1 lb	4 cups
Smoked ham, diced	100 g	4 oz	1 cup
Curry powder	5 ml	1 tsp	1 tsp
Salt	5 ml	1 tsp	1 tsp
Eggs, beaten	2	2	2
Spring onions (scallions), finely chopped	3	3	3
Salted peanuts	25 g	1 oz	¼ cup

① Heat the wok or a large heavy-based frying pan (skillet).

② Pour in the oil and when hot add the rice and stir-fry for about 2 minutes.

③ Add the ham to the pan and cook for 30 seconds.

④ Stir in the curry powder and salt, then the beaten eggs and stir for about 2 minutes or until the egg is set.

⑤ Serve hot with the spring onion and peanuts sprinkled over.

PREPARATION TIME: 5 MINUTES
COOKING TIME: 6 MINUTES

CREAMY MUSHROOMS AND PRAWNS

—— SERVES 4 ——

	METRIC	IMPERIAL	AMERICAN
Oil	15 ml	1 tbsp	1 tbsp
Garlic clove, crushed	1	1	1
Shallot, finely chopped	1	1	1
Button mushrooms, quartered	225 g	8 oz	8 oz
Cooked prawns (shrimp)	225 g	8 oz	8 oz
Paprika	2.5 ml	½ tsp	½ tsp
Soured (dairy sour) cream	150 ml	¼ pt	⅔ cup
Salt and freshly ground black pepper			

① Heat the wok or a large heavy-based frying pan (skillet).

② Pour in the oil and when hot stir-fry the garlic and shallot for 30 seconds.

③ Add the mushrooms and cook for about 2 minutes.

④ Stir in the remaining ingredients. Heat through and serve.

PREPARATION TIME: 5 MINUTES
COOKING TIME: 4 MINUTES

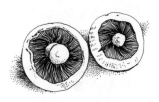

MEDITERRANEAN BRUSCHETTA

—— SERVES 4 ——

	METRIC	IMPERIAL	AMERICAN
Medium French stick	1	1	1
Oil	15 ml	1 tbsp	1 tbsp
Garlic cloves, crushed	2	2	2
Spanish onion, finely sliced	1	1	1
Large red (bell) pepper, cut into fine rings	1	1	1
Large yellow or orange pepper, cut into fine rings	1	1	1
Tomato purée (paste)	30 ml	2 tbsp	2 tbsp
Can of anchovies, drained	100 g	4 oz	1 small
Black olives, stoned (pitted)	12	12	12
Chopped fresh oregano or marjoram	15 ml	1 tbsp	1 tbsp
Salt and freshly ground black pepper			

① Slice the French stick in half lengthways, then cut each half into two.

② Heat the wok or a large heavy-based frying pan (skillet).

③ Pour in the oil and when hot add the garlic and stir-fry for a few seconds.

④ Add the onion and peppers and stir-fry for 2 minutes until soft.

⑤ Add the tomato purée, anchovies, olives and herbs and heat through, stirring, for about 1 minute.

⑥ Season, then pile the mixture on the bread and serve.

PREPARATION TIME: 10 MINUTES
COOKING TIME: 5 MINUTES

SALMON WITH EGG NOODLES

—— SERVES 4 ——

	METRIC	IMPERIAL	AMERICAN
Oil	15 ml	1 tbsp	1 tbsp
Garlic clove, crushed	1	1	1
Spring onions (scallions), finely chopped	4	4	4
Mangetout (snow peas)	50 g	2 oz	2 oz
Precooked medium egg noodles, drained	350 g	12 oz	12 oz
Can of pink salmon, drained	215 g	7½ oz	1 med
Lemon juice	15 ml	1 tbsp	1 tbsp
Chopped fresh parsley	15 ml	1 tbsp	1 tbsp
Salt and freshly ground black pepper			

① Heat the wok or a large heavy-based frying pan (skillet).

② Pour in the oil and when hot add the garlic and spring onions and stir-fry for 30 seconds.

③ Add the mangetout and cook for 1 minute.

④ Stir in all the remaining ingredients, ensuring that they are well combined, heat through and serve.

PREPARATION TIME: 5 MINUTES
COOKING TIME: 5 MINUTES

SUMMER TOMATOES AND BEANS

—— SERVES 4 ——

	METRIC	IMPERIAL	AMERICAN
Oil	15 ml	I tbsp	I tbsp
Spring onions (scallions), sliced	3	3	3
Large ripe tomatoes, skinned, seeded and sliced	450 g	I lb	I lb
Can of flageolet beans, drained	300 g	I I oz	I large
Shredded fresh sweet basil leaves	30 ml	2 tbsp	2 tbsp
Lemon juice	15 ml	I tbsp	I tbsp
Sugar	5 ml	I tsp	I tsp
Extra virgin olive oil	5 ml	I tsp	I tsp
Salt and freshly ground black pepper			

① Heat the wok or a large heavy-based frying pan (skillet).

② Pour in the oil and when hot add the spring onions and tomatoes and cook for 1–2 minutes so that the tomatoes are starting to soften but still retain a little shape.

③ Stir in the beans and basil leaves and cook for a further 30 seconds.

④ Add the remaining ingredients, seasoning to taste, and serve hot or cold.

PREPARATION TIME: 10 MINUTES
COOKING TIME: 4 MINUTES

BACON AND MUSHROOM STIR-FRY

—— SERVES 4 ——

	METRIC	IMPERIAL	AMERICAN
Oil	15 ml	1 tbsp	1 tbsp
Thick smoked bacon, diced	350 g	12 oz	12 oz
Button mushrooms, quartered	175 g	6 oz	6 oz
Cherry tomatoes	100 g	4 oz	4 oz
Worcestershire sauce	10 ml	2 tsp	2 tsp
Salt and freshly ground black pepper			
Buttered toast			

① Heat the wok or a large heavy-based frying pan (skillet).

② Pour in the oil and heat, then add the bacon and fry (sauté) for 2–3 minutes or until it has changed colour.

③ Add the mushrooms and stir-fry for 1 minute.

④ Stir in the tomatoes and Worcestershire sauce and cook for 1 minute, then season to taste.

⑤ Serve with buttered toast.

PREPARATION TIME: 5 MINUTES
COOKING TIME: 7 MINUTES

SPICED LAMB POCKETS

—— SERVES 4 ——

	METRIC	IMPERIAL	AMERICAN
Plain (all-purpose) flour	15 ml	1 tbsp	1 tbsp
Curry powder	5 ml	1 tsp	1 tsp
Ground cumin	2.5 ml	½ tsp	½ tsp
A pinch of ground cinnamon			
A pinch of chilli powder			
Salt and freshly ground black pepper			
Boneless lamb, cut into fine strips	350 g	12 oz	12 oz
Oil	30 ml	2 tbsp	2 tbsp
Lemon juice	15 ml	1 tbsp	1 tbsp
Large pitta breads	4	4	4
Mango chutney	60 ml	4 tbsp	4 tbsp
Crisp lettuce leaves, finely shredded	4	4	4
Small onion, finely sliced	1	1	1

① Combine the flour with the spices and salt and pepper and use to coat the lamb.

② Heat the wok or a large heavy-based frying pan (skillet).

③ Pour in the oil and when very hot add the lamb and stir-fry for about 4 minutes until it is tender and slightly crisp on the outside, then stir in the lemon juice.

④ Lift the lamb out of the pan with a draining spoon and keep warm.

⑤ Split the pitta breads and spread 15 ml/1 tbsp of the chutney in each.

⑥ Divide the lettuce, onion and lamb between the pitta breads and serve hot.

PREPARATION TIME: 10 MINUTES
COOKING TIME: 6 MINUTES

SPICED CHICK PEAS

—— SERVES 4 ——

	METRIC	IMPERIAL	AMERICAN
Dried chick peas (garbanzos)	175 g	6 oz	1 cup
Oil	90 ml	6 tbsp	6 tbsp
Salt	5 ml	1 tsp	1 tsp
Chilli powder	5 ml	1 tsp	1 tsp
A pinch of ground cumin			
A pinch of sugar			

① Soak the chick peas in cold water for at least 4 hours, preferably overnight, then drain.

② Heat the wok or a large heavy-based frying pan (skillet).

③ Pour in the oil and when very hot add the chick peas and stir-fry for about 2–3 minutes until they are crisp and lightly browned.

④ Transfer to a bowl with a draining spoon and, while they are still very hot, mix in the salt, spices and sugar.

⑤ Serve cold as a side dish or as nibbles with drinks.

PREPARATION TIME: 3 MINUTES PLUS SOAKING
COOKING TIME: 4 MINUTES

Variation: Use a can of chick peas, rinsed and drained, as a quick alternative.

CARAWAY CAULIFLOWER WITH PARMA HAM AND CHEESE

—— SERVES 4 ——

	METRIC	IMPERIAL	AMERICAN
Cauliflower	350 g	12 oz	12 oz
Oil	30 ml	2 tbsp	2 tbsp
Small onion, finely chopped	1	1	1
Caraway seeds	15 ml	1 tbsp	1 tbsp
Parma ham, cut into fine strips	100 g	4 oz	1 cup
Cream cheese	100 g	4 oz	½ cup
Salt and freshly ground black pepper			

① Cut the cauliflower into very small florets and shred any thick stems.

② Heat the wok or a large heavy-based frying pan (skillet).

③ Pour in the oil and when hot add the cauliflower and onion and stir-fry for about 4 minutes or until both are quite tender.

④ Add the caraway seeds and ham and cook for 30 seconds.

⑤ Stir in the cream cheese and cook until it has melted. Season to taste, mix well and serve hot.

PREPARATION TIME: 10 MINUTES
COOKING TIME: 7 MINUTES

CURRIED EGGS WITH SMOKED HADDOCK

—— SERVES 4 ——

	METRIC	IMPERIAL	AMERICAN
Oil	15 ml	1 tbsp	1 tbsp
Small onion, finely chopped	1	1	1
Mild curry powder	5 ml	1 tsp	1 tsp
A pinch of turmeric			
A pinch of ground cumin			
Large tomatoes, skinned and chopped	2	2	2
Single (light) cream	30 ml	2 tbsp	2 tbsp
Natural yoghurt	30 ml	2 tbsp	2 tbsp
Smoked haddock, cut into thick strips	350 g	12 oz	12 oz
Hard-boiled (hard-cooked) eggs, quartered	4	4	4
Salt and freshly ground black pepper			
Chopped fresh coriander (cilantro)	5 ml	1 tsp	1 tsp

① Heat the wok or a large heavy-based frying pan (skillet).

② Pour in the oil and when hot add the onion and cook for 2–3 minutes until soft.

③ Stir in the spices and cook for 30 seconds.

④ Add the tomatoes, cream and yoghurt and cook, stirring, for about 2 minutes until heated through.

⑤ Finally, gently stir in the fish and eggs and cook for 2–3 minutes only, to ensure that the fish is done. Season to taste.

⑥ Serve with the coriander sprinkled over the top.

PREPARATION TIME: 10 MINUTES
COOKING TIME: 10 MINUTES

PRAWN AND POTATO FRITTATA
—— SERVES 4 ——

	METRIC	IMPERIAL	AMERICAN
Oil	30 ml	2 tbsp	2 tbsp
Small red onion, chopped	I	I	I
Parboiled potato, diced	225 g	8 oz	8 oz
Cooked prawns (shrimp)	225 g	8 oz	8 oz
Chopped fresh parsley	15 ml	I tbsp	I tbsp
Salt and freshly ground black pepper			
Eggs, beaten	4	4	4

1. Heat the wok or a large heavy-based frying pan (skillet).
2. Pour in the oil and when hot add the onion and cook for about 1 minute.
3. Add the potato to the pan and stir-fry for 1 minute, then stir in the prawns and parsley and cook for a few seconds.
4. Season to taste, then pour the eggs over and reduce the heat very slightly. Do not agitate the eggs but allow to set for a few minutes to form a thick omelette.
5. Turn the omelette over and allow to set.
6. Cut into thick chunks and serve hot or cold.

PREPARATION TIME: 5 MINUTES
COOKING TIME: 10 MINUTES

HAM AND COURGETTES WITH FETA

—— SERVES 4 ——

	METRIC	IMPERIAL	AMERICAN
Oil	15 ml	I tbsp	I tbsp
Shallot, finely chopped	I	I	I
Courgettes (zucchini), cut into thin, short sticks	2	2	2
Thick ham, finely cubed	350 g	12 oz	3 cups
Feta cheese, crumbled	100 g	4 oz	I cup

① Heat the wok or a large heavy-based frying pan (skillet).

② Pour in the oil and when hot add the shallot and cook for 30 seconds.

③ Add the courgettes to the pan and stir-fry for about 3 minutes or until they soften slightly.

④ Stir in the ham and cook briefly to heat through.

⑤ Spoon the mixture into individual bowls and sprinkle the feta cheese on top while still very hot.

PREPARATION TIME: 10 MINUTES
COOKING TIME: 6 MINUTES

DESSERTS

The wok is not generally associated with the preparation of desserts, but it can be an excellent vessel in which to prepare very simple yet mouthwatering desserts to impress dinner guests.

Be adventurous with stir-frying fresh fruits in mild oil, then adding a splash of wine or liqueur, or make a syrup at the last minute by adding butter, sugar and golden (light corn) syrup to the wok. These creations are excellent served with either ice cream or chilled cream. Cubes of firm cake or bread also make a good basis for a dessert, but take care not to break them up when turning them in the pan. These can be greatly enhanced by the addition of grated chocolate and nuts at the final stages of cooking.

The key to creating successful desserts in the wok is to ignore tradition and experiment with textures, flavours and colours!

CHOCOLATE AND PECAN MELT
—— SERVES 4 ——

	METRIC	IMPERIAL	AMERICAN
Oil	15 ml	1 tbsp	1 tbsp
Chocolate sponge cake, cut into small cubes	225 g	8 oz	8 oz
Pecan nuts, halved	50 g	2 oz	½ cup
Plain (semi-sweet) chocolate, grated	50 g	2 oz	½ cup
Marshmallows	50 g	2 oz	2 oz
Crème fraîche	60 ml	4 tbsp	4 tbsp

1. Heat the wok or a large heavy-based frying pan (skillet).

2. Pour in the oil and when hot add the cake and stir-fry for 1–2 minutes until slightly crisp on the edges.

3. Add the nuts and cook for 1 minute.

4. Stir in the grated chocolate and marshmallows and cook until all the chocolate has melted and the marshmallows are just starting to melt.

5. Pile into four individual serving dishes and top each with 15 ml/1 tbsp crème fraîche.

PREPARATION TIME: 5 MINUTES
COOKING TIME: 5 MINUTES

HOT ORANGES WITH CHESTNUTS

—— SERVES 4 ——

	METRIC	IMPERIAL	AMERICAN
Oil	15 ml	1 tbsp	1 tbsp
Canned shelled chestnuts, sliced	100 g	4 oz	4 oz
Large oranges, peeled, segmented and membrane removed	3	3	3
Icing (confectioners') sugar	15 ml	1 tbsp	1 tbsp
Fresh orange juice	30 ml	2 tbsp	2 tbsp
Cointreau	15 ml	1 tbsp	1 tbsp

① Heat the wok or a large heavy-based frying pan (skillet).

② Pour in the oil and when hot add the chestnut slices and stir-fry for about 2 minutes or until they are lightly browned.

③ Add the orange segments and cook for 1 minute.

④ Stir in the sugar, juice and Cointreau, heat the mixture through and serve hot.

PREPARATION TIME: 15 MINUTES
COOKING TIME: 5 MINUTES

CHERRIES WITH SWEET MELBA CROÛTONS

—— SERVES 4 ——

	METRIC	IMPERIAL	AMERICAN
Thick slices of white bread	3	3	3
Egg, beaten	I	I	I
Icing (confectioners') sugar	15 ml	I tbsp	I tbsp
Ground cinnamon	7.5 ml	1½ tsp	1½ tsp
Oil	30 ml	2 tbsp	2 tbsp
Can of stoned (pitted) cherries, drained and syrup reserved	410 g	14½ oz	I large
Sugar	10 ml	2 tsp	2 tsp
Chilled cream or yoghurt, to serve			

1. Discard the crusts and cut the bread into 2.5 cm/1 in cubes.

2. Combine the egg, icing sugar and cinnamon and pour over the bread cubes. Mix well and leave to soak for 10 minutes.

3. Heat the wok or a large heavy-based frying pan (skillet).

4. Pour in the oil and when hot add the bread cubes and stir-fry for 1–2 minutes until brown and crisp all over.

5. Stir in the cherries, 30 ml/2 tbsp of the reserved syrup and the sugar and heat through for a few seconds.

6. Serve hot with chilled cream or yoghurt.

PREPARATION TIME: 3 MINUTES PLUS SOAKING
COOKING TIME: 4 MINUTES

HONEYED EXOTIC FRUITS
—— SERVES 4 ——

	METRIC	IMPERIAL	AMERICAN
Medium pineapple	½	½	½
Oil	15 ml	1 tbsp	1 tbsp
Sesame seeds	30 ml	2 tbsp	2 tbsp
Mango, peeled, stoned (pitted) and cubed	1	1	1
Nectarine, stoned and sliced	1	1	1
Seedless grapes	50 g	2 oz	2 oz
Kiwi fruits, peeled and thickly sliced	2	2	2
Clear honey	45 ml	3 tbsp	3 tbsp

① Skin and core the pineapple and cut the flesh into 2.5 cm/1 in cubes.

② Heat the wok or a large heavy-based frying pan (skillet).

③ Pour in the oil and when hot add the sesame seeds and cook for a few seconds.

④ Add all the fruit and stir-fry for about 3 minutes.

⑤ Stir in the honey, heat through and serve hot.

PREPARATION TIME: 20 MINUTES
COOKING TIME: 5 MINUTES

PEACHES WITH SWEET WHITE WINE
—— SERVES 4 ——

	METRIC	IMPERIAL	AMERICAN
Oil	15 ml	I tbsp	I tbsp
Fresh peaches, skinned, stoned (pitted) and sliced	4	4	4
Sweet white wine	90 ml	6 tbsp	6 tbsp
Ground almonds	30 ml	2 tbsp	2 tbsp
Icing (confectioners') sugar	15 ml	I tbsp	I tbsp
Flaked (slivered) almonds, lightly toasted	30 ml	2 tbsp	2 tbsp

①   Heat the wok or a large heavy-based frying pan (skillet).

②   Pour in the oil and when hot add the peach slices and gently stir-fry for about 5 minutes or until they are tinged brown.

③   Add the wine and cook for a minute or so to reduce the amount of liquid slightly.

④   Stir in the ground almonds and icing sugar and cook for 1 minute.

⑤   Serve hot, topped with the flaked almonds.

PREPARATION TIME: 5 MINUTES
COOKING TIME: 9 MINUTES

MADEIRA BANANAS WITH BUTTERSCOTCH SAUCE

—— SERVES 4 ——

	METRIC	IMPERIAL	AMERICAN
Oil	15 ml	1 tbsp	1 tbsp
Madeira cake, cut into small cubes	100 g	4 oz	4 oz
Small bananas, sliced	4	4	4
Walnut pieces	50 g	2 oz	½ cup
For the sauce:			
Soft brown sugar	30 ml	2 tbsp	2 tbsp
Granulated sugar	30 ml	2 tbsp	2 tbsp
Butter	30 ml	2 tbsp	2 tbsp
Golden (light corn) syrup	15 ml	1 tbsp	1 tbsp
Double (heavy) cream	75 ml	5 tbsp	5 tbsp

1. Heat the wok or a large heavy-based frying pan (skillet).
2. Pour in the oil and heat, then add the cake, bananas and walnuts and stir fry for 1–2 minutes or until the cake is slightly tinged brown on the edges.
3. Remove the banana mixture from the pan and keep warm.
4. To make the sauce, place all the ingredients except the cream in the wok and stir until they have completely melted and combined.
5. Stir in the cream and heat through.
6. Serve the banana mixture in individual bowls with the sauce drizzled over.

PREPARATION TIME: 5 MINUTES
COOKING TIME: 6 MINUTES

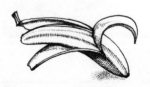

SPICED PUMPKIN STIR-FRY
—— SERVES 4 ——

	METRIC	IMPERIAL	AMERICAN
Pumpkin	450 g	1 lb	1 lb
Oil	15 ml	1 tbsp	1 tbsp
Pecan nuts, halved	75 g	3 oz	¾ cup
Ground cinnamon	2.5 ml	½ tsp	½ tsp
Grated nutmeg	2.5 ml	½ tsp	½ tsp
Golden (light corn) syrup	15 ml	1 tbsp	1 tbsp
Brown sugar	15 ml	1 tbsp	1 tbsp
Water	60 ml	4 tbsp	4 tbsp

① Peel and seed the pumpkin and cut the flesh into 1 cm/½ in cubes.

② Heat the wok or a large heavy-based frying pan (skillet).

③ Pour in the oil and when very hot stir-fry the nuts for about a minute or until they are browned.

④ Add the pumpkin to the pan and stir-fry for 4–5 minutes until it has softened slightly.

⑤ Add the remaining ingredients, cover the pan and reduce the heat slightly.

⑥ Simmer for about 3–4 minutes until the pumpkin is tender but not mushy. Serve hot.

PREPARATION TIME: 10 MINUTES
COOKING TIME: 10 MINUTES

HOT LEMON SQUARES

—— SERVES 4 ——

	METRIC	IMPERIAL	AMERICAN
Lemon juice	45 ml	3 tbsp	3 tbsp
Plain lemon or madeira cake, cubed	225 g	8 oz	8 oz
Oil	30 ml	2 tbsp	2 tbsp
Lemon curd	45 ml	3 tbsp	3 tbsp

①　Pour the lemon juice over the cake and leave to soak for 10 minutes.

②　Heat the wok or a large heavy-based frying pan (skillet).

③　Pour in the oil and when hot add the cake and stir-fry for 1–2 minutes so that the cake is slightly browned at the edges.

④　Gently stir in the lemon curd so that the cake does not break up, heat through and serve hot.

PREPARATION TIME: 2 MINUTES PLUS SOAKING
COOKING TIME: 4 MINUTES

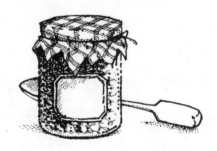

PEARS WITH CINNAMON AND SEEDS
—— SERVES 4 ——

	METRIC	IMPERIAL	AMERICAN
Oil	30 ml	2 tbsp	2 tbsp
Pumpkin seeds	15 ml	1 tbsp	1 tbsp
Sunflower seeds	15 ml	1 tbsp	1 tbsp
Sesame seeds	15 ml	1 tbsp	1 tbsp
Pears, peeled, cored and thinly sliced	3	3	3
Soft brown sugar	25 ml	1½ tbsp	1½ tbsp
Lemon juice	15 ml	1 tbsp	1 tbsp
Ground cinnamon	15 ml	1 tbsp	1 tbsp
Chilled cream or yoghurt, to serve			

① Heat the wok or a large heavy-based frying pan (skillet).

② Pour in the oil and when hot add all the seeds and stir-fry until they are crisp but not burnt – this should take only a few seconds.

③ Add the pears and cook for 1 minute.

④ Carefully stir in the sugar, juice and cinnamon being careful not to break the pear slices. Heat through.

⑤ Serve with chilled cream or yoghurt.

PREPARATION TIME: 3 MINUTES
COOKING TIME: 4 MINUTES

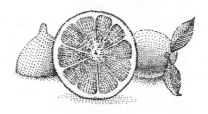

SWEET POLENTA

—— SERVES 2 ——

	METRIC	IMPERIAL	AMERICAN
Water	400 ml	14 fl oz	1¾ cups
Lemon juice	60 ml	4 tbsp	4 tbsp
Coarse-grain cornmeal	100 g	4 oz	1 cup
Finely grated lemon zest	60 ml	4 tbsp	4 tbsp
Brown sugar	30 ml	2 tbsp	2 tbsp
Honey	60 ml	4 tbsp	4 tbsp
Ground cinnamon	10 ml	2 tsp	2 tsp
Ground cloves	5 ml	1 tsp	1 tsp
Plain (all-purpose) flour	20 ml	4 tsp	4 tsp
Oil	60 ml	4 tbsp	4 tbsp
Greek-style natural yoghurt	120 ml	4 fl oz	½ cup

① Bring the water and lemon juice to the boil in a saucepan and shower in the cornmeal.

② Whisk the mixture constantly until it thickens and starts to leave the sides of the pan.

③ Stir in the lemon zest, sugar and half the honey, then pour the mixture into a shallow container lined with clingfilm (plastic wrap).

④ Chill the polenta in the refrigerator for at least 1 hour.

⑤ Turn the polenta out of the dish and cut into 2.5 cm/1 in cubes.

⑥ Mix together the cinnamon, cloves and flour and use to coat the cubes.

⑦ Heat the wok or a large heavy-based frying pan (skillet).

⑧ Pour in the oil and when hot stir-fry the cubes in small batches for 1–2 minutes until slightly browned all over.

⑨ Lift out the cubes with a draining spoon and divide between two dessert bowls.

⑩ Top the cubes with the Greek yoghurt, then the remaining honey and eat immediately.

PREPARATION TIME: 20 MINUTES PLUS SETTING
COOKING TIME: 6 MINUTES

BRANDY APPLES

—— SERVES 4 ——

	METRIC	IMPERIAL	AMERICAN
Oil	30 ml	2 tbsp	2 tbsp
Firm eating (dessert) apples, peeled, cored and sliced	750 g	1½ lb	1½ lb
Brandy	30 ml	2 tbsp	2 tbsp
Icing (confectioners') sugar	45 ml	3 tbsp	3 tbsp

① Heat the wok or a large heavy-based frying pan (skillet).

② Pour in the oil and when hot add the apple slices and cook for 3–4 minutes until they are slightly tender and tinged brown.

③ Pour on the brandy and cook for several minutes to evaporate some of the brandy.

④ Dredge with the icing sugar and serve hot.

PREPARATION TIME: 10 MINUTES
COOKING TIME: 8 MINUTES

WHISKY BREAD PUDDING
—— SERVES 4 ——

	METRIC	IMPERIAL	AMERICAN
Thick slices of white bread	4	4	4
Egg, beaten	I	I	I
Whisky	25 ml	I ½ tbsp	I ½ tbsp
Mixed (apple-pie) spice	10 ml	2 tsp	2 tsp
Single (light) cream	65 ml	4½ tbsp	4½ tbsp
Oil	30 ml	2 tbsp	2 tbsp
Demerara sugar	30 ml	2 tbsp	2 tbsp
Sultanas (golden raisins)	30 ml	2 tbsp	2 tbsp
Raisins	I5 ml	I tbsp	I tbsp

① Discard the crusts and cut the bread into 2.5 cm/1 in cubes.

② Combine the beaten egg, whisky, mixed spice and 25 ml/1½ tbsp of the cream and pour over the bread cubes. Mix well and leave to soak for 10 minutes.

③ Heat the wok or a large heavy-based frying pan (skillet).

④ Pour in the oil and when hot stir-fry the soaked bread cubes for 1–2 minutes until they are browned on all sides.

⑤ Drain off any excess oil, then quickly stir in the remaining cream, the sugar and dried fruit.

⑥ Heat through for a few seconds, then serve hot.

PREPARATION TIME: 5 MINUTES PLUS SOAKING
COOKING TIME: 3 MINUTES

INDEX